THROUGH THE WAVES:

Life and Business Stories of
Captain Kim Jae-chul

THROUGH THE WAVES :
Life and Business Stories of Captain Kim Jae-chul
by Gong Byung-ho

Cover design by Studio LES
Design edited by EwhanD&B(+82-2-2254-4301)
Edited by Sunho Shin, Junehee Jeong, and Ewhan D&B
Supervised by Eun-gui Chung
Printed by NEO printech(+82-2-718-3111)
published in Republic of Korea by HUINE, an imprint of Hankuk University of Foreign Studies University Knowledge Contents and Press, Seoul.
http://press.hufs.ac.kr
First printing, 2019. 7. 31
ISBN 979-11-5901-592-2 04800
979-11-5901-590-8 (Set)
Price 9,000 Won

THROUGH THE WAVES:

Life and Business Stories of Captain Kim Jae-chul

Gong Byung-ho

HU:iNE

The History of Dongwon Group - by Gong Byung-ho

In dedication to Captain Kim with love and respect of HUFS

Upon the Release of the Abridged Version

During his 20s, Kim Jae-chul once shared the following lesson that he learned on the job. "Passion is not something you chase after, but something that naturally follows when you work hard. A path will open up in front of you when you work hard at something you have already started, rather than spending a lot of time deciding which path to take."

In particular, he always stresses that "Leaders must know more, work harder and make greater sacrifices than their subordinates."

The incredible life of Kim Jae-chul has given hope and courage to many young people and helped leaders across a diverse range of fields realize the importance of humility and wisdom. If I were asked to recommend a single book that could serve as a life model for young people in Korea, I would choose this book without hesitation. Furthermore, I am certain that this book will serve as a living textbook for business majors and those who dream of starting their own business. I would once again like to pay tribute to Chairman Kim Jae-chul.

This edition was produced as an abridged version of the Biography of Kim Jae-chul as part of the Ilgok Cultural Foundation's 'Building a Brighter Future' campaign. I would like to express my gratitude to the author, who has fully adopted the spirit of the foundation, as well as the president of 21st Century Books and Hwasan Munhwa for their help in printing the abridged version.

This abridged edition is based on the Biography of Kim Jae-chul
(Written by Gong Byung-ho, published by 21st Century Books, 813 pages)

December 15, 2016 Choi Jae-seon,
Director of the Ilgok Cultural Foundation

Prologue

Captain Kim, a Life of Navigating Tall Waves

Mountainous waves crash against the ship as if they will swallow it up, sending huge volumes of water spilling across the deck. In the face of the fierce waves, the skipper and helmsman on the bridge can barely see an inch in front of them as the sea swirls around them like a torrent from hell.

The ship perilously climbs to the crest of the wave, only to be plunged once again into the trough of the 10 meter swell. The deafening crash and splintering shock as the ship hits the bottom of each wave cause the supplies of cabin to fall, tossed and thrown about. What could be going through the captain's mind at this time? Kim Jae-chul, who made a name for himself in his younger days as the captain of a deep sea fishing vessel, speaks in a calm voice.

"If I returned home alive, I resolved to live a clean and dignified life since I was living on borrowed time. When you manage to live through a critical situation, you become a completely different person."

Those that emerge victorious from in any era will always face challenges and enjoy both moments of success and moments of frustration. Those from the previous generation in Korea lived through a very special time in modern Korean history.

As recently as the early 1960s, rural villages in Korea would experience food shortages every spring and go through a prolonged period of hardship, which led to a prevailing sense of resignation. However, at a time of deeply entrenched poverty, the Korean people were lucky enough to be offered an opportunity to escape from poverty through systematic hard efforts.

1961 was the year in which Korea began its long journey towards industrialization. It was a time when the entire nation strived as one under the rallying cry of 'Let's live the good life.' The people who lived through that era have heart wrenching stories of tears and sorrow that would fill several volumes.

The Life of a Man Who Walked the Boundary Between Life and Death Countless Times

This book is the story of a man who was born as the eldest of 11 children in a poor rural village and fought to escape from poverty that he was destined to be trapped in.

The formative years of Kim Jae-chul, the founder of Dongwon Group and Korea Investment Holdings, were the mid-1950s to the 1960s. This was a period in which Korea began to rise from the ashes of the Korean War.

There are many stories about great entrepreneurs in this world, but the biography of Kim Jae-chul holds a special kind of value. While the majority of entrepreneurs remain firmly rooted on land, deep sea fishing in the vast ocean is a completely different story.

A person who has escaped many brushes with death will naturally come to hold a unique worldview.

Kim Jae-chul earned himself a reputation as 'Captain Kim' while working as the skipper of vessels in the South Pacific and Indian Oceans during his early 20s. He is an integral part of the history of Korea's deep sea fishing industry, and his life story is not limited to events of the past. This story also speaks to the present and the future.

This book is not simply an account of the growth of one man, but also a record and appraisal of the sacrifices made by the previous generation to make it through an era of hardship and build a livable country. I hope that those living in the present era will also renew their resolve to build a better country in the future.

February 2016

Gong Byung-ho (Author)

Contents

Part I

The Vestiges of Life

story 1

A Fateful Encounter

Memories from His Hometown of Gangjin

Kim Jae-chul was born in Naedong Village in Gundong-myeon, Gangjin County in Jeollanam-do on March 30, 1934. Naedong Village was located approximately 10kilometers north of Jeong Yak-yong's House of Dasan. Kim recalls the first time he came into contact with the ocean.

"I was in third grade at elementary school. I heard that someone had caught a big turtle at the beach more than 20 miles from my house in my hometown, and I ran there on the way home from school because I really wanted to see what it looked like. It was a huge turtle. I was so busy taking everything in that the day was gone before I knew it. I wasn't able to go home that day, and stayed up all night wide awake under the stone wall of a nearby house. I can still remember the scolding I got from my parents when I went home the next day."

Who could have guessed that the sea, which Kim first came across during this fateful encounter, would come to serve as the greatest stage in his life? Perhaps we can catch a glimpse of this in the fact that Kim was always a curious boy who could never let something go once it piqued his interest.

Fishing was something he enjoyed growing up, and it was the nearby Tamjin River that gave him this opportunity. Kim loved to observe and catch the fish, and dive in and out of the water.

He finished his schooling at Gundong Elementary School in 1947, then passed through Gangjin Middle School before graduating from Gangjin Agricultural High School in 1954. Gangjin Agricultural High School was 5km from his house, so Kim had to walk 10kilometers every day on his way to and from school. Walking such a long distance was tough, but it helped him to build up a strong level of fitness that would serve him well throughout life. He used to think to himself as he walked, and had deep conversations with nature.

Kim was never absent throughout his six years of middle and high school. He often got up at dawn to help with farm and household chores before going to school. At the time, practical experiences accounted for half of the curriculum in agricultural high schools, and it was during this period that Kim attempted to start his first business. He planted watermelons in the 3,000 square meter field near Tamjin River, and the large harvest caused a sensation in the town.

When I asked Kim how he was able to grow watermelons so successfully, he replied, "Based on what I had learned in school, I tried to come up with even better methods and worked hard. After school I went to the fields and worked until the stars came out."

A Positive Legacy Left by His Father

Most people say that they view the world through the standards they came to acquire as children. I was able to learn that there are several things which have not changed in

Kim's life as well. Many of them were heavily influenced by his father.

Kim's father, Kim Gyeong-muk (1914-1991), was a hard worker but struggled to make ends meet. Kim Jae-chul was the eldest of seven sons and four daughters living under one roof. Similar to most adults of his time, Kim Gyeong-muk had never received a formal education and learned most of what he knew in a village schoolhouse. However, he studied on his own and was always reading newspapers and books. He was a renowned intellectual to the extent that people often sought him out for a comment or tidbit of knowledge about anything that was happening in the village.

"My father was not an educated man, but he had amazing willpower," Kim recalls. "When he was young, he resolved to never touch cigarettes or alcohol, and stuck to that his entire life." His father was a strong believer in independence and the spirit of self-help. He repeatedly reminded his children that they should 'never depend on anyone else' and that 'people should know their place in life.'

Before he passed away, Kim Gyeong-muk quietly called his son over and handed him five million KRW. "When I go, I want you to use this money to buy a large ox and treat everyone in the neighborhood," he said. He did not want to be indebted to anyone, even his eldest son.

Like his father, Kim Jae-chul adopted independence and the spirit of self-help as important guiding principles in his life. He also acquired the knowledge and skills he needed to adapt to any situation, which served him well throughout life.

As a child, Kim Jae-chul often heard other adults in the village remark "Everything will turn out okay for you kids, because your father has built up a lot of goodwill." The other virtue that Kim Gyeong-muk engrained in the minds of his children was "No matter how valuable something is, it is more virtuous to share it with others than keep it to yourself."

"My father always rode around on a bicycle. Whenever he was greeted by a young person or child, he would stop and get off his bike to greet them properly." The principle of treating others as valuable was later reflected in Kim Jae-chul's management philosophy of investing in his staff.

"Did you ever imagine that so many people would fill the streets to pay tribute to the memory of your father?" After

Kim Gyeong-muk passed away in Seoul, a sea of elderly people carrying linen a mile long, and men and women of all ages were waiting when the funeral hearse arrived in his hometown. A line of mourners that extended for hundreds of meters walked around Gangjin to lament his death.

Although he had lived the life of an ordinary villager, several hundred people came out to see him off. Kim Jae-chul says that he still vividly remembers that scene. In 2014, 23 years after his passing, the people in Kim Gyeong-muk's hometown erected a monument in his honor to pay tribute to the 'golden man.'

Dear Mother

The life of Kim's mother also had a large influence on her son. The person who provided Kim's father with the greatest help to be an ideal paternal figure was his mother. She had great respect for her husband. Whenever she stayed at the house of one of her sons or daughters, she never placed her own clothes on top of those of her husband's as a sign of respect. She was always attentive to her husband.

Kim's mother showed her children how to treat other people through her actions. Her life can be summarized by the words 'responsibility' and 'patience.'

Kim Jae-chul's birth home was located about one kilometer from his elementary school, and athletics day at the school was treated as a celebration, with almost every parent in the village participating. However, Kim's mother was so busy that she never had time to attend the event. Other mothers prepared food and enjoyed the atmosphere of athletics day along with their children. He must have felt sad about not having his mother around on those special days.

When Kim Jae-chul's siblings grew up and had children of their own, they realized how much their mother had done for them to be busy to the extent that she was unable to attend the annual athletics day.

At the time, women in rural areas were expected to make clothes for their families, cook, pound rice using a mortar, carry heavy goods to the market and back, fetch water and also tend to the fields. They rose at dawn, worked until past midnight and weaved whenever they found time. Women also had numerous children, and because children were unable to be weaned off breastfeeding until the age of three, they were mere physical laborers until one of their sons married and a daughter-in-law arrived that could be delegated some of the work.

The following is 'A Letter to my Mother' written by Kim Jae-chul on his mother's 99th birthday.

Mother!

The most admirable mother in the world! The children that you raised through hard work and sacrifice have gathered together to celebrate your 100th birthday.

You have really achieved something amazing. From marrying into a dirt-poor family, looking after the family burial grounds and sacrificing everything for your family and children, you have lived a truly honorable life.

As we were growing up, you worked in the fields during the day, then collected vegetables in the evening to sell at the market 10 miles away at dawn in order to pay for our schooling. You toiled away every day while the 11 of us attended elementary school, unable to attend the school athletics day even once!

At the time, we were resentful because we were too young to understand. I remember how you were also a master of hiding food. When we returned home from school hungry for a snack, we couldn't find anything even after turning the entire kitchen and shed inside out.

Your children have now become grandparents. Even Jae-un, who used to eat sake cake and get drunk when he was poor, and Jae-guk, who you would comfort with ripe persimmon that you had hidden somewhere when he refused to leave your side. Jae-sun, who was often late for school after helping out in the kitchen, is now in his 60s, and even I, your eldest son who you always thought was so fragile, am past the age of 70.

A lot of time has passed.

I remember how you looked when you were younger, as you worked all day without taking a single break. That image is still fresh in my mind.

I believe that the reason we were able to grow up and live happy lives, despite coming from a situation of hardship, is the dedication you and my father demonstrated while raising us, and the fact that you always stressed the importance of honesty, diligence and independence. This is why the respect I feel for you and my father continues to grow every day.

Mother! You are truly a remarkable woman. Thanks to your love, we grew up happy and healthy, and you now have dozens of grandchildren and great-grandchildren who are all growing into brave young men and women.

You no longer need to worry about us, and your children and grandchildren hope that you live a long and healthy life.

Mother! I wish you the best of health.

Written by Jae-chul on an auspicious day in February 2012

An Era in Which Time Passed Slowly

Ever since he was young, Kim Jae-chul would always write down a sentence on the first page of his diary at the beginning of each new year.

"Life is better as your burden becomes heavier, because this allows you to grow."

It is a quote from Tokugawa Ieyasu.

Kim always carried a deep sense of responsibility to seek a better life for both himself and his family.

Kim Nam-goo, the eldest son of Kim Jae-chul, says that even when he was attending university, the thought of carrying on his father's business had never crossed his mind. "How can someone work that hard in life? My father's life is too difficult. Why should I live like that?"

There was an incident which caused Kim Nam-goo to change his mind and take on a strong sense of responsibility. Shortly before graduating college, he was on a trawl-boat in the northern seas, and that experience caused him to feel the same sense of responsibility his father carried in the depths of his heart. Kim Jae-chul made his eldest and second sons promise one thing before joining the business. He told them that leaders must be willing to take responsibility and make sacrifices.

Jung Byeong-seon, who spent six years in middle and high school with Kim Jae-chul, said that during the two hour walk to and from school along the fieldside path, Kim would spend his time memorizing English vocabulary while the other kids chatted amongst themselves. He is impressed that Kim still carries the same attitude today.

As I conducted interviews for this book, there were many occasions on which I was overwhelmed with emotion, wondering how it was possible for a person to live such a devoted life.

Meeting a True Teacher

Up until he left his hometown, the area around Gangjin was all that Kim Jae-chul knew of the world. He went to great lengths to ensure that he and his family could live in comfort. As he saw the state of the poor rural villages, Kim became certain that the path towards prosperity for Korea was bringing more wealth to those villages. Thanks to his outstanding grades, Kim had already received a scholarship and decided to study at Seoul National University's College of Agriculture. However, at that point something unbelievable happened.

It was fate

Kim Jae-chul met Choi Seok-jin (former professor at Chonnam National University's College of Engineering, 1928-2004), who was the teacher in charge of the third grade at the time. Originally from Yeongam County, Choi had been admitted to Seoul National University's College of Liberal Arts and Sciences in 1949, and worked at Gangjin Agricultural High School for five years since his sophomore year in 1951. Meeting Choi turned out to be a great blessing for Kim.

The young teacher believed that it was his duty to guide students down the correct path in life. He founded a boy scouts group, and even wrote and composed a song for the club. Perusing the lyrics of this song gives the impression that Kim was very fortunate to have met Choi at a point in life when he was thinking about his future career.

1. The growing young men in the boy scouts
Are buoyed by the spirit rising in the east over Wolchulsan Mountain
The sound of a baby's cry at birth, that promises a better future
Let us discover hope and march forward

2. The surging waves in the west brush past the hearts
Of the growing young men in the boy scouts
Let us look towards the day where infinite promise
Comes together to form a strong bond, and charge forward

The lyrics offer a glimpse into how the 25 year-old teacher must have nurtured the spirits and dreams of his students. It is notable that the 'Dongwon Family Song' that Kim Jae-chul personally wrote in 1970 faithfully embodies the same spirit and dreams that Choi instilled in his students.

1. The flag of Dongwon flies high in the sky
Unfurling across the five oceans and six continents
Unfolding its wings towards a glorious tomorrow

There is great reward to be found in the joy of every workplace
(Chorus)
We are gathered together on the roots of belief
Let's do something grand and embrace the world
Let that name ring out forever, Dongwon family

2. Dongwon's mission of earnest corporate activities
The world is a stage on which we dash forward
New days appear before us through passion and challenge
There is honor to be found in every new workplace
(Chorus)

One day in the lead up to Kim's graduation, when the students were thinking hard about their futures, Choi told his students a story that would serve as an important life lesson.

"I'm not going to tell you to go to an elite university. Although I am attending Seoul National University myself, I'm still arguing with you absurdly. You need to be able to look wider and deeper and design your own life. If I were you, I would follow a path that leads to the ocean. Korea is surrounded by the ocean on three sides, and I believe that Korea has the potential to develop into the best nation on earth, but this depends on the extent to which young people strive to explore the ocean."

Up to 60 students listened to this story, but it was only in the mind of Kim Jae-chul that his teacher's advice planted a seed which began to grow.

"Sir, which university should I attend if I want to head to the ocean?"

"I'm not entirely sure, but I think there are colleges in Busan."

Great opportunities come along by chance, but it only takes an instant to grasp them. Kim acted immediately, and that opportunity became the starting point for a dramatic change in his life.

At the time, there were two educational institutions related to the sea in Busan - Busan National Maritime University (currently Pukyong National University) and Korea Maritime and Ocean University. Kim hurried to submit an application to these maritime universities. His father expressed his discomfort with the decision, saying "I can send you rice, but you will have to catch the fish to make side dishes yourself since you will be at sea."

As recently as the late 1970s, the word 'baetnom' (literally 'boat guy') was used in Korea as a less than flattering term for sailors. As a top student, the people at school also had plenty to say about Kim's sudden change of heart.

Rather than complimenting Kim for venturing into unexplored territory, most people reacted with a mix of disappointment and sarcasm, saying "He says he's going to a baetnom school."

Kim's life entered a new phase once he made the decision to study at a maritime university. The bond with his lifelong mentor continued, and Choi became a director at the Dongwon Educational Foundation once he retired from working at Chonnam National University.

Kim has since thanked Choi on several occasions, saying that he made him who he is today.

story 2

Chasing an Ambitious Dream at Sea

Leaving Home

Kim Jae-chul left his beloved home on a cold winter day in February 1954. This was the first time he had left his hometown and stood on his own two feet. Hunched up in a third-class cabin on a coastal liner, he struggled to fall asleep. He felt a sense of anticipation about his new life, but this was mixed with anxiety. He had decided to roll the dice of fate.

Considering the fact that Kim's hometown only gained access to electricity several years after he left, the bright lights of Busan as seen from the passenger ship must have been an incredible surprise to the young man, who had only just turned 20.

Let's take a look at what was going on in Busan in the 1950s. Busan had served as the temporary capital of Korea since the year in which the Korean War broke out, but this role came to an end in August 1953. It was only six months later when Kim Jae-chul arrived in Busan. The city was filled with refugees and facing a critical housing shortage. Makeshift shacks had been erected in any and every available space. With two friends, Kim made his home in a small shack located at the top of a mountain slope in Yeongdo.

At the time, Busan National Maritime University was located in Namhang-dong, Yeongdong-gu. However, the new students who had been looking forward to superb campus facilities were disappointed by the makeshift buildings (barracks) on campus. When it rained, the bare floor school buildings would flood with water, and the chilling Yeongdo sea breeze in winter would make the classroom so cold that the ink dried up. The maritime university students who spent their youth in such conditions later played a crucial role in Korea's deep sea fishing industry.

The money that Kim's family sent to him was not enough

to cover his expenses. However, he did not ask for more. "When I went to college, I originally thought that I would be able to deliver newspapers or work as a private tutor. Since there are a lot of institutions related to the maritime industry, I thought that many of them would be interested in receiving newspapers, but when I got there I realized that those institutions were very far away. It was impossible to deliver to them. And people had no interest in hiring the country people from Jeolla-do as private tutors. I had to think long and hard about what I could do."

Kim took on any job or errands he could find, juggling his studies with part-time work. In his sophomore year, his younger brother Jae-un finished middle school in Gangjin and came to Busan.

Kim, who was 22 at the time, stayed in the mountainside shack with his two friends and his 18 year-old brother. Kim asked his brother. "You said you were earning money while attending school, so what do you plan to do now?" "Anything is fine with me, so I was hoping you could look into a job I can do," he replied.

Looking back on that time, Jae-un recalled "Thanks to

my brother's timely help, I was able to get a job working in a weapons supply depot as a laborer for 175 KRW per day." Jae-un often had to work at night, so Kim Jae-chul moved to a location that was closer to his brother's workplace. Gamman-dong, where his brother worked, was on the opposite side of the sea from Yeongdo, which meant that Jae-chul had to take the ferry to Busan City Hall and then cross Yeongdo Bridge in order to get to school and back.

While he was in college, Kim Jae-chul worked hard to find a way to make a living. Around this time, he was able to grasp a special opportunity.

When an influx of Koreans living abroad flooded into Busan after Korea's liberation from colonial rule, the government implemented several policies to solve the housing crisis. Those without a place to stay were granted a small plot of land on which they could build their own house. However, some people took advantage of this policy to sell the land instead of building a house. After becoming aware of this opportunity, Kim saved his tuition money up to buy two plots of land. At first, he had planned to use the land to raise chickens, but later changed his mind and bought construction materials to build a house whenever he had time away from his studies. This was made possible through desperation and need.

"I spent almost no money at all. The plot of land was on a mountainside, so I had to level it. My brother and I dug so hard with pickaxes that it made sparks fly, and it was really difficult because of the slope. While I was building the house I mainly subsisted on pulbbang, a kind of Korean pancake dumpling. Looking back now it seems ridiculous, but at the time I could do it because I was young. Once the house was finished, I lived there for 18 months before stepping aboard a deep sea fishing vessel." The hard work paid off, and the completed house looked better than many other homes in the area.

Kim says that some of the local kids would even scribble 'rich man's house' on the front door. The house, which was Kim's first major achievement in life, is still owned by Dongwon Industries.

Finding a Direction in Life

"The whole country was poor, so for most college students there was very little of the freedom or romance that you see today."

Students have few memories of their days in college because they spent most of the time juggling studies and work. However, for Kim Jae-chul there were many 'firsts' during that time, including one that took place while he was at the maritime university.

In July 1957, the Ministry of Education (currently the Ministry of Education and Science) approved a new plan for final year students at the university to board a training ship and engage in practical marine training in waters near Taiwan. Forty eight students from the Fishing Department boarded the boat, and a grand ceremony was held to see them off. The ship was a 103 ton wooden training vessel called the Hongyang, and the training was to take place over 19 days. In fact, the ship was originally a Japanese vessel that had been captured by the Korean government for crossing the 'Syngman Rhee Line' (peace line).

At the time, traveling abroad was something that average Koreans could only dream about, and it was unheard of for college students to go overseas for a training session. Per capita income was only $50 in Korea at the time, and presidential approval was required for exchanging even $100.

One of the most memorable parts of the training was catching a 2.7 meter, 50 pound marlin that was offered to President Syngman Rhee as a gift. The university news channel ran a piece about a 'marlin at the Blue House,' which captured the surprised look on the face of the president and his aides when they saw the fish.

By coincidence, a ship called the Jinam that had been catching tuna in the Indian Ocean as part of a pilot project crossed paths with the training vessel in Keelung Harbor. This was the beginning of Kim's special relationship with tuna. Later on, he volunteered to work on the Jinam I's training voyage to the South Pacific in January 1958.

While Kim was attending college, the future of near sea fishing looked bleak due to the depletion of fish stocks, and he began to regret his decision to study at a maritime university. In 1957, a year before he was set to graduate, Kim was offered a teaching position by his former principal at Gangjin Agricultural High School who had become the new principal at Yeosu Maritime High School. If Kim had chosen the safe route at that time, he would never have become the star of this book.

1958, the year of Kim's graduation, also saw the advent of deep sea fishing in Korea. After successfully conducting a test operation, Shim Sang-ju, the president of Jedong Industries, sent the Jinam to Samoa to begin catching tuna full-time. When Kim read the story in a newspaper, he decided that he wanted to be on that ship.

Captain Yoon Jeong-gu, who was in charge of hiring the crew for the voyage, stated that he would give priority to those who had experience on fishing vessels in the Indian open, followed by those who had longline fishing experience.

There was no room left for a 24 year-old with no experience to speak of. However, Kim put everything on the line boldly out of the firm belief that this opportunity could change his life.

It was determination, rather than fate, that played a larger role in Kim Jae-chul's career path. Kim made the surprising decision to volunteer as an unpaid apprentice officer. This may have been the first time that a maritime college graduate had started his deep sea fishing career as an ordinary crew member instead of a deck officer.

A Special Connection to the Jinam

In January 1958, the Jinam set sail for Samoa under the leadership of Captain Yoon, with 18 crew on board. Kim, who had only narrowly made it onto the ship, was the first graduate of a maritime university to work on a deep sea fishing vessel as a regular member of the crew. Also on board the 12 year-old ship was Moon Je-an from the Hankook Ilbo, one of the Korea's very first reporters. In the first article submitted by Moon, he wrote about the hard work put in by the Jinam crew members to pioneer the deep sea fishing industry in the face of difficult conditions.

Jinam was set to sail 5,000 miles over a period of seven to eight months of navigating tall waves and looking over nothing but endless horizons of the Pacific Ocean to catch tuna. The voyage of Jinam was not only critical as a source of revenue for Korea's economic reconstruction, but also historically significant as it would mark the start of a new chapter in Korea's offshore fishing history. In particular, as my first time being onboard a fishing vessel, there was not a single thing that ever failed to amaze me nor give me thrills. And all the backwardness of the nation that we experienced during the journey and what we had to do desperately to overcome it were a sorrowful struggle that brings tears.

"When we entered the port at Shimonoseki in the early morning, we could see black smoke bellowing from the chimneys of dozens of factories in the Kitakyushu industrial region, which filled us with envy."

The stark contrast between the level of development in Korea and Japan left a strong impression on 24 year-old Kim Jae-chul, who had never seen a proper industrial chimney before in his life. At the port, the crew loaded extra fishing gear onto the ship and purchased bait that would be used for catching tuna. However, they ended up staying for another week due to an engine malfunction.

At the time, Kim received an allowance of approximately $5, and used the money to buy stacks of secondhand illustrated books on fish that were sold in bundles according to weight. Since Kim had been a third grader in elementary school at the time Korea was liberated, he had been forced to learn a little bit of Japanese. He later became fluent in the language, which was of great help in growing his business.

After setting sail from Shimonoseki, the Jinam arrived in Samoa on January 30, exactly one month after departing from Busan. While most of the crew spent their days playing cards, Chinese chess or Mahjong, Kim studied Japanese and read the books he had bought to learn more about fish, including tuna.

The ship picked up six additional crew members in Samoa, then headed towards the fishing grounds on February 26, casting the first nets two days later on February 28. At the time, up to 53 Japanese fishing vessels were in Samoa. Captain Yoon recalls that he "could think of nothing but the fact that if we failed, I would be ruined, the company would go bankrupt and it would be a national disgrace."

Kim was keen to learn and worked hard at every task he was assigned, including not only fishing itself, but cleaning the toilets, swabbing the deck and running small errands, as well as other work that he sought out of his own accord. Since he learned everything from the ground up, Kim was equipped with a detailed knowledge of every aspect of the trade when he later became a captain and business owner.

There was a joke between crew members that the ship belonged to the ship owner while it was on land, but belonged to the captain when it was at sea. This demonstrates the immense power wielded by the captain. If the ship owner did not have a solid understanding of the fishing trade, there was great potential for him to be swayed by the captain. Many ship owners who jumped into the deep sea fishing industry later made an inglorious exit from the stage, and a lack of knowledge about the business was one of the main reasons.

Over a 12 month period in Samoa, the Jinam ventured out to fish six times, catching 450 tons of tuna that was supplied to Van Camp's for $90,000. By the standards of those times, this was a significant sum of foreign currency. After spending 12 months on the ship as an unpaid officer, Kim returned home safely in February 1959.

Buoyed by the success of the first fishing expedition,

Jedong Industries sent two additional vessels, the Jinam II and Jinam III, to Samoa in May of 1959.

On this occasion, Kim joined the crew as a first officer, receiving a monthly salary of $200. The two vessels returned to Korea in July 1960 and April 1961, with successful hauls that earned $90,000 and $150,000 respectively. Even after coming home, Kim maintained a special connection with the Jinam as he pursued his dreams.

Youthful Experiences that Money Can't Buy

"Passion is not something you chase after, but something that naturally follows when you work hard. Rather than spending a lot of time deciding which path to take, the path will open up when you do your best at something you have started." This was the lesson that Kim Jae-chul learned while working as an unpaid crew member.

"At that time, everyone was rushing into the tuna business because they heard it was profitable. But no one had any hands-on experience. I was the first person with an undergraduate degree to actually experience life on a ship.

The two years I spent at sea catching tuna became a great asset for me."

Kim's fascination with studying books about fish and researching tuna fishing, which first began in Shimonoseki, carried over into other parts of his life.

A Captain's Dream Comes True in Samoa

The Jinam I, on which Kim worked as an unpaid crew member, had been bought in 1949 with $320,000 in American aid. President Syngman Rhee named it the Jinam (literally 'pointing south') to signify "Turning the bow of the boat towards the Southern Ocean and dredging wealth from the sea."

The Jinam II and Jinam III had also been paid for with $150,000 in aid from the US, but they were 80-ton fishing vessels commissioned from a Japanese shipyard for the purpose of catching tuna. At the time, there was a dire shortage of captains capable of handling tuna vessels, which presented Kim with a great opportunity.

Becoming the Captain of Jinam II

He was selected as the captain for the Jinam II. The main reason for his appointment was the work ethic he had displayed over the previous two and a half years, and the fact that he had direct experience working on fishing vessels. Although he was seemingly too young to be a captain, the ship owner had no choice but to appoint him. Kim became the captain of the Jinam II at the young age of 26.

In January 1961, the Jinam II set sail for Samoa under the leadership of Captain Kim, with 23 crew members on board. The ship reached its destination three weeks later. The vessel returned to Korea in May 1962, with Kim having demonstrated superb competence as a leader.

Kim trained his skills as a captain in the fishing grounds of Samoa, later earning the nickname 'Captain Kim' or simply 'J.C. Kim.' He was able to bring in large hauls of fish for several reasons.

① He was not caught up in the conventional wisdom followed by the majority, and had the wisdom and courage to make his own decisions on where to fish. At the time, most of the Japanese vessels were gathered in the fishing grounds located to the northwest of Samoa. However, during his time in Samoa Kim chose to fish in the grounds to the east, which are about to enter the peak season, located near the 160th meridian west of the Cook Islands. Of course, this decision was made after conducting thorough research beforehand.

② He relied on his unique fishing technique and knowledge gained from first-hand experience. "It is impossible to see schools of fish in the vast ocean with the naked eye. If flocks of sea birds such as seagulls are catching anchovies or horse mackerel from the sea, it means that tuna are also spawning nearby, as they seek out the same food."

③ He made the right calls in each situation, and never let down his guard. Kim stressed the importance of sticking to one's principles while also remaining flexible.

④ He took steps to prevent accidents and used both sticks and carrots to get the most out of his crew. Kim had a mild temperament, but also demonstrated strong leadership by not shying away from reprimanding employees or applying strict rules when necessary. The foundations of this leadership lay in Kim's habit of closely observing people ever since he first served as a crew member.

⑤ He taught the new fishing techniques he had learned to his crew through repeated training.

When Kim returned to Korea with a massive haul, the Dong-a Ilbo ran an article the following day that read "Jinam II returns with a catch of $130,000··· flying high with a massive haul."

> "According to Kim, the captain of the ship, which had left Busan on January 7, 1961, over a period of 13 months after arriving in Samoa on February 1, they caught 550 tons of tuna worth $140,000 in 9 voyages in an enormous fishing ground of over 3,000 miles in radius and sold them to a local food company before leaving. Jinam II sent $120,000 to Korea after the expenses for food for 21 crew members and fishing gear. He said with confidence that he could earn so much more money as long as he could keep going back out there fishing."

This article was the first time that the world had heard the name Kim Jae-chul. The diary that Kim kept on board also offers a glimpse into the situations he faced and the role and tribulations of a captain. He wrote "I have to let people know through writing, so that more Koreans will take an interest in the sea." Kim's thoughts and actions demonstrated remarkable poise for a young man in his 20s! Contributing articles to newspapers, giving interviews and creating and releasing charts to the public were all part of Kim's efforts to make Korea a richer country.

This propensity later led Kim to take a great interest in Konosuke Matsushita. At one point, he even looked into the viability of setting up a Matsushita Institute in Korea. Even now, Kim continues to dream about projects to support his country and seeks ways to put these plans into action.

A Life of 'Daily Improvement'

Kim Jae-chul wrote the following entry in his diary on January 7, 1961.

> After several months of unstable living in my homeland, it feels refreshing to be heading back out to the raging sea. When I came back to my cabin after sailing past the Oryukdo Islands and checking that the ship was in good working order, I suddenly felt heavily fatigued, and a faint tinge of sadness from all the farewells prior to departure. Being unable to get a good night's sleep for several days while preparing for the voyage, the tear-stained faces of those who came out to bid us farewell, and the sight of my crew members silently waving goodbye to their families. (...)

After Kim transferred to another company, the Jinam II, the first ship that he had captained, sunk off the coast of Samoa while fishing. All 21 crew members lost their lives in the accident. At the time, Kim was fishing nearby on a vessel called the Donghwa I. Although he rushed to the aid of the distressed ship along with six other vessels, they were unable to find any survivors.

The development of the deep sea fishing business was accompanied by numerous casualties like this, particularly in the early days. This was because companies had no choice but to employ old fishing vessels.

In the ten year period from 1958, up to 90 men lost their lives in the fishing grounds off the coast of Samoa. Kim

Jae-chul was able to stare death in the face and live to tell the tale. In 1971, a White Whale Tower was erected on the campus of the maritime university to pay tribute to the souls who passed away at sea. The words engraved on the statue remind people living in the current era of abundance about how the previous generation strived to build the Korea of today.

Great Spirits
Are they listening to the sound of bells
That echoes through the campus
In the Pacific Ocean and Indian Ocean
In the North seas and the South Pacific
In oceans around the world
Our heroic boys from the Maritime University

Who fought with the sea waves and their lives like patals
Their noble cause embedded in the hearts of every generation
Today, we rose as a cairn in this place
That stands and looks out to sea

Have a safe journey
Our sons of the sea
Let the courageous sailors
Stay with us forever

Kim Jae-chul wrote the following entry in his diary on January 25, 1961.

> "The crew have laid out an awning on the deck to play Go and Chinese chess. After we left port, I became fond of reading and spent my time reading the books I bought in Japan."

He once told me this story. "People often ask me how I managed to write my own speeches, but when I was going through my old records, I was able to confirm the fact that I read a lot of thick books, including Marx, Engels and Rousseau during that time. I think that reading a lot taught me writing skills that would last a lifetime. It not only helped me think clearly and run my business more systematically, but also helped me look far into the future."

Although he was only a young captain, Kim's on-board diary offers a glimpse into what qualities he thought a leader should possess.

January 28
The crew members who are on their maiden voyage seem to be anxious because they haven't seen a single island in more than two weeks since we passed a sandbank. Even those who are on their second voyage are saying "Last time we saw an island after a few days, why can't we see any this time?" I imagined what would have happened if they had been on Columbus' ship. (…)

March 7
We have been working through the night for a week after casting the first longline. It takes four hours to cast the longline and 15 hours to haul it in, so we are working almost 20 hours a day. The crew are sleep-deprived, and no one can keep their eyes open. Some of them even doze off while holding the line outside in heavy rain. I know that it is a tough ask, but in this situation we cannot allow ourselves to be weak. The crew often get discouraged on days when we don't bring in a good catch. It's tough for me as well on those days, but knowing to put on a brave face in front of the crew

and act with hope and conviction is the wisdom and spirit that a captain must embody.

March 10
The hot, sticky weather makes us feel even more exhausted. Even worse, today a killer whale ripped into the fish we had caught and ate them all, so we have nothing to show for our hard work. When performing grueling work, lifting the haul onto the ship brings a sense of comfort and boosts morale, but the crew are down on themselves and in a sorry state today. The brutal ordeal for a skipper on his maiden voyage continues. (…)

An Effective Way to Overcome Adversity

You must be able to emerge victorious in crucial moments. If there are tough days, there will also be good days. Kim Jae-chul kept a diary that recorded his life at sea because he was always cognizant of this. On March 15, five days after the crew had become discouraged, the fishing conditions greatly improved.

"The fiery sun shined on our faces for the first time in ages. As the sea calmed down, casting the longline became a lot easier and we finished around midnight. We caught four tons today, and we feel like winners after catching some big fish. The crew have started smiling once again."

Kim learned at sea that sunshine always comes after the rain. Although people will work hard for their personal benefit, they are willing to sacrifice and dedicate themselves even more for a greater cause. At the time, there were 50 or so Japanese vessels fishing in the waters near Samoa, and only three Korean ships. The young men were obsessed with beating the Japanese. Kim's strong will to win can be seen in his diary entry from March 25.

"Today we have a full ship. The Japanese boats that arrived with us are still fishing. With a full boat, I feel relieved that we have been able to follow in the footsteps of our predecessors, and delighted that we surpassed the Japanese ships. In the first half of this voyage, we went through a rough time with foul weather, frequent engine problems and a number of illnesses. But everything turned for the better, and today we can celebrate. At 11 p.m., we steered the heavily laden ship towards Samoa.

A Diary of Romance and Dreams

On March 26, on the way back to the port in Samoa after completing his first voyage as a captain, Kim wrote the following entry in an emotional moment.

> "The boat is so full that the deck is below the waterline, and water spills over onto the deck. There is almost no wind today, and the wake on the quiet seas leaves a long trail like a contrail in the autumn sky."

Even at the young age of 27, Kim had the ability to describe the world in a poetic detail. At the time, the Dong-a Ilbo reported on Kim's activities with an article titled 'All about the Fishing Grounds of Samoa in the South Pacific' that described Samoa, how important it was, and how three Korean fishing vessels had managed to outcompete the Japanese ships.

In 1963, the year that Kim turned 29, he returned to Samoa as the captain of the Donghwa I. At the time, there were 70 or so Japanese vessels and 30 Korean ships fishing in the waters near Samoa. When Kim once again returned to port with the largest haul, a grand farewell banquet was held in his honor by StarKist, the company he was supplying, before his ship set sail for Korea.

This led to a disgruntled response from some Japanese fishermen who complained that Kim was being treated to a farewell banquet when they had been working hard to supply fish for several decades and never received such treatment.

However, StarKist had a good reason to be grateful to Kim. He was the first captain to supply the company, and his large haul had saved StarKist from a shortage of raw materials.

The Korean Deep Sea Fishing Industry in the Early 1960s

As recently as the 1960s, the Korean economy was largely dependent on aid from the US. The first five year economic plan was implemented in 1962, and with the government' s hard work to earn as many dollars as possible, Korea recorded exports of $100 million in 1964. This figure exceeded $180 million in 1965, with marine products accounting for 16% of the total, of which deep sea fishing exports made up 8.5%.

The revolutionary government, that came to power at a time when Korea had no industrial base to speak of, began to look towards the deep sea fishing industry as a means of obtaining more foreign currency and securing food security. Accordingly, the proportion of marine product exports occupied by deep sea fishing began to skyrocket from 1966. From 19% in 1966, the figure climbed to between 30 and 40% over the following three decades.

The man who spearheaded exploration of the deep sea fishing market was Shim Sang-jun, the head of Jedong Industries. With his unique way of thinking and broad network of overseas connections, Shim made a substantial contribution to the development of the Korean deep sea fishing industry.

When word spread that there was money to be made in the deep sea fishing business, a host of new companies rushed to enter the industry. Materials from that period show that there were ten Korean vessels fishing near Samoa including five ships from Jedong Industries, two from Hwayang Leading Company, one from Hannam and two from Donghwa in 1964, as well as another ten vessels in the

Indian and Atlantic oceans. The number of deep sea fishing vessels continued to grow, reaching 65 in 1965, 152 in 1967 and 850 by 1977.

The rapid growth in the industry led to skyrocketing demand for captains, and Kim Jae-chul was well equipped to take advantage of this trend. However, among the numerous companies that jumped into the industry to be a part of the gold rush, only a tiny fraction stood the test of time.

After returning to Korea with a full haul on the Jinam II in May 1962, Kim transferred to Donghwa, one of Jedong Industries' competitors. At the time, the captain and crew signed contracts for a year at a time, with the net profit split 60/40 between the ship owner and crew. Kim decided to leave the Jinam because of difficulties obtaining the share of the profits he had been promised for delivering results.

Nevertheless, he still referred to Shim Sang-jun as the 'godfather of deep sea fishing,' a clear acknowledgment of the important role Shim had played in getting Korea's deep sea fishing industry off the ground.

After leaving Jedong Industries, Kim began sailing as the captain of the Donghwa I. He served at sea for 12 months before spending 20 months on land. The reputation of 'Captain Kim' grew even further after he traveled to Samoa as the head of the fleet and captain of the Donghwa I, returning with a substantial haul.

Executives at other companies in the industry tried everything they could to headhunt Kim Jae-chul. Kim later worked at the struggling Goryeo Susan for ten months, and helped to 'steady the ship.'

At the time, Goryeo Susan had dispatched ten deep sea fishing vessels to the South Pacific, with some of the captains hailing from marine colleges. After being recruited as a department head at Goryeo Susan, Kim gave plenty of advice to CEO Eo Yoon-il.

"Marine college graduates are experts in merchant vessels. Expertise in fishing vessels and expertise in merchant shipping are fundamentally different. If you continue to put together crews like this, it will only lead to greater losses. You need to change this practice immediately," he said, and produced financial reports on the profitability of each ship.

When he heard this, dark clouds suddenly began to form in Eo's eyes. Having jumped into the deep sea fishing business after hearing it was profitable from a friend, Eo was bewildered by what he was hearing. Kim also learned a lot from hearing about the mistakes that executives had made through rumors or stories.

Later in life, Kim always made an effort to verify things through a variety of channels and listen to the minority opinion when making decisions, and this was largely due to the knowledge he gained from observing management failures.

His Wife, a Reliable Ally

Kim Jae-chul returned to Korea from his voyage on the Jinam II in May 1962, and left Busan Port on the Donghwa I in January 1963. During the period in between, he got married and started a family.

When I asked him about his wife, he replied "She is a traditional woman from a Confucian household, and a good wife and wise mother. She doesn't say much, but she always understands me."

While his wife expressed respect for her husband by

building him up in front of their children, Kim expressed his love by protecting her from the rough elements of the world. When confronted with difficulties outside the home, Kim would alleviate his wife's concerns by telling her that he had the situation under control. While Kim shared good news with his wife, he tended to endure hardships on his own.

In the same way as Kim's mother had cared for his father, his wife had a similar disposition to her mother-in-law. "You are a noble man. You are really something," she would say to him, offering words of encouragement. She always seemed to know what was on his mind. She expressed her respect for Kim to their children as well, saying "Korea would be a different place if there were more people like your father in this world." This demonstrates the firm trust that existed between the two of them.

story 3

A Gift from the Sea

Leading the Fleet that Pioneered Fishing Grounds in the Indian Ocean

In the 1960s, captains of deep sea fishing vessels were akin to modern-day athletes in that they had to prove their worth through results. After the ship owner had made a huge investment and taken on substantial risk, the performance of the ship ultimately depended on the captain's ability. This led to great competition between ship owners to attract competent captains to their vessels, as a good captain could be the difference between success and bankruptcy.

Korea Wonyang Fisheries was established in 1963. The

company built a 230-ton tuna fishing vessel, then obtained a further ten ships in 1966. Seven of these vessels were dispatched to the South Pacific, with the other three sent to the Indian Ocean. CEO Lee Hak-su had a background in the publishing business, so there was no way he could know the ins and outs of the deep sea fishing industry. Instead, he worked hard to find a person who could handle things on his behalf. After setting his sights on Kim Jae-chul, Lee set about persuading him to join the company.

In 1965, Kim finally agreed to serve as the head of the Fishing Division at Korea Wonyang Fisheries at the age of 30.

On the Frontier of Indian Ocean Exploration

Korea Wonyang Fisheries' newly-constructed vessels the Gwangmyeong IX, X and XI were sent to the Indian Ocean in 1965, with Kim serving as the captain and head of the fleet.

At the time, Kim's decision to directly participate in the voyage left many people scratching their heads. They wondered why he would give up a cushy job on land to risk his life by once again heading out to sea. However, Kim thought differently. He believed that the ocean was the place where he could fulfil his ambitions.

On-board Diary from the Indian Ocean

After leaving Busan Port on April 2, 1966, the Gwangmyeong arrived in the Indian Ocean on May 5. Kim continued to faithfully write entries in his diary. Some of his diary entries about the challenges and successes he faced between May 8, when the ship first entered the Indian Ocean, and July 7, when the vessel sailed into Durban Port in South Africa with a full haul, have been been published in nationwide school textbooks in Korea.

The diary entries offer insight into the young man's inner world as he served as the head of the fleet and captain of the Gwangmyeong VI, as well as detailed descriptions of the sea and fishing conditions.

May 8

This morning the sea is burning with passion. The horizon in the east was dyed a beautiful color, and the majestic crimson sun abruptly rose into the sky. The calm seas are teaming with fish, and seagulls of all sizes swooped down to greet the morning waters. The vast ocean, the glaring rising sun, and the schools of flying fish leaping out of the water! The harmony of nature is truly spectacular. (…)

May 12
We fished for the first time in waters 300 miles south of Ceylon on the 7th day after leaving Penang. This was a test operation to try out our new fishing gear and learn about the tuna in this area. The crew had nervous expressions on their faces nervous since this is our first day, and at dawn I too wished for a good haul and a safe return.

At 4am, the quiet sea shines brightly in the reflection of moonlight, creating a mysterious glow. As soon as I gave the order to prepare for casting the longline, the working lamps in hundreds of cabins lit up and the crew were deployed to their respective places under the glaring lights. When I gave the order to begin casting, the crew tossed the hooks baited with frozen mackerel pike into the ocean. The reel and line began to slide over the edges of the boat as we steamed ahead.

A flock of seagulls were surprised by the rapidly moving ship, and flew behind us, following the lights. The crew, also hoping for a great catch, were buoyed by this as if they too were seagulls hunting for fish. Over four hours, we set a line with more than 2,000 baited hooks across a 35-mile area. After casting was complete, we waited four hours before beginning to reel in the line from midday, under the burning sun.

The hooks were pulled onto the boat one by one as we turned the reel. With a mix of anticipation and disappointment, this was met with cries of "There's fish!"

When the tuna finally gave up their stubborn fight and relented, they were pulled to the sides of the boat and quickly hauled on board with hooks. One large tuna was 1.5 meters long and weighed more than 50 kilograms. Its fin had a yellowish hue, so we named it Yellow Fin. (…)

May 26

Porpoises are causing us a lot of trouble, so we gave up on the central fishing grounds and began sailing towards the grounds in the southwest of the Indian Ocean, where the water temperature is lower. (…)

No matter how good a spot may be, it is ruined as soon as a pod of porpoises shows up.

June 6

We began fishing to the south of Africa at a latitude of 31 degrees south and a longitude of 35 degrees east. Unlike in the central fishing grounds, the seas here are rough, with howling waves, a water temperature of 22 degrees and almost no days with good weather. But as it is close to winter, the waters are teaming with albacore that are migrating south to the Indian Ocean from the

Atlantic, so many foreign vessels are here fishing alongside us.
I was worried because I am unfamiliar with this spot, but thankfully the ocean currents are not too fast. As predicted, we keep hauling in scores of yellowfin, which caused more cries of joy on the ship. (…)
With the crew's shouting and the howling of the waves, the boat has been rocking all day like a pirate ship. With almost 200 yellowfin and dozens of other fish, our haul today is close to three tons. On the final day, we reeled in a 250 kilogram swordfish. As the sun goes down, the wind picks up and the boat is rocked by mountainous waves, but the crew are intoxicated by the thrill of today's catch and animatedly talk amongst themselves. (…)
We finished working late at night and began chasing the next school of tuna so that we can cast the line again tomorrow.

July 6
We finally have a full boat. Although a lot of our hard-earned tuna catch was stolen by pods of dolphins or sharks, we have caught about 7,000 fish. It is even more gratifying because this is the first time we have filled our ship in the Indian Ocean. We received messages of congratulations from other ships that we were communicating with, and received notice that the Gwangmyeong IX and X, which were fishing near to us, also have a full catch.
If the joy of sailing lies in entering port, the joy of fishing lies in a full boat. We have reeled in our fishing gear and are racing towards port. The crew held a celebratory party on the sides of the

ship. "Let's go to sea, let's go to sea, let's go to the sea of surging waves..." Burned bright red from the sun, the crew sang in chorus, which brought the atmosphere on board to pitch fever and helped everyone momentarily forget how tired they were. The joy of sailing to port with a full boat must feel similar to a victorious admiral returning home with the spoils of war. With 120 tons caught over 40 casts, the first voyage was a success. With this achievement, the Korean deep sea fishing industry reached another milestone in the Indian Ocean.

July 7
As the day grew light, the African continent came into view, and the smell of earth filled our nostrils. When I look back, the waves of the Indian Ocean are still tall, and the beacon atop the port lighthouse is still shining brightly in the early morning. We arrived at Durban Port in the Republic of South Africa. (...)

Exploring New Fishing Grounds in the Indian Ocean

Although it was in Samoa that Kim Jae-chul had made a name for himself as an outstanding captain, his fleet achieved great success in the Indian Ocean. People's jaws dropped at the sight of a 230-ton ship returning to port with a haul of 120 tons. The Gwangmyeong X had caught 120 tons, with the Gwangmyeong IX bringing in 110 tons.

At the time, Japan was experiencing a boom in premium fish such as tuna sashimi buoyed by the country's rapid growth. The fish caught in the Indian Ocean were loaded onto a 5,000 ton refrigerated carrier and then divided between ten freight ships that began the long journey to Japan.

At this point, it is worthwhile to note the difference between the fishing grounds in the South Pacific and those of the Indian Ocean. In the South Pacific, fishing vessels mainly catch albacore which are used for canned products, while the Indian Ocean is home to bigeye tuna and yellowfin, which are used in raw fish dishes.

During this period, Japanese vessels would often keep an eye on the movements of Kim Jae-chul and follow his ship around. Whenever this happened, Kim would say "There are plenty more good fishing grounds out there" and seek out a new location. The Japanese fishermen could not hide their surprise when they saw the heavily laden Korea Wonyang Fisheries ships return to port after quickly catching a full haul. Kim's success led to booming business for Korea

Wonyang Fisheries.

Over ten voyages, Kim earned $1.17 million in export revenue. This is an astronomical sum compared to the industry average at the time. In 1967, Kim earned $1.68 million across 17 voyages. The fleet of three ships that headed out to the Indian Ocean in 1966 had grown to 14 ships by 1969.

In relative terms, how much was the $1.17 million earned by Kim's fleet? Korea's per capita income, which was only $125 in 1966, had grown to $31,705 by 2015. With per capita income growing 253 times over the period, Kim's haul would be valued at $300 million today. This demonstrates how deep sea fishing was the top earner of foreign currency in Korea.

After working on the seas for a year, Kim returned to Korea in March 1967. Images of Kim arriving at Gimpo Airport wearing a Burberry coat can be found in faded newspaper articles. He was now 33, and at the time he was promoted to a member of the company board, others who were seven or eight years senior to Kim were still working as deputy department heads.

Filling Gaps in One's Knowledge through Learning

"If there is gap in your knowledge, fill it through learning. If something must be done, give it your best shot. Whatever the task, work hard and seek to go above and beyond."

These are the deeply rooted beliefs that Kim Jae-chul held dear ever since a young age, and also a promise that he made with himself. When he began fishing in the Indian Ocean, Kim's results were not spectacular, even accounting for the superior experience and knowledge of the Japanese vessels. However, he continued to put in effort to learn the fishing methods of the Japanese ships and improve his equipment.

"He studied every aspect of the Japanese ships. The Japanese vessels used lines that were close to 80 km in length. In a location where the other ships couldn't see, he would briefly pull up their lines to measure the size of their hooks and compare them to ours. We also had a stronger will than the Japanese fishermen. If they cast 2,000 baited hooks then we would cast 2,500, so of course we were able to land a greater haul. He would always have a sonar detector turned on to track the movements of fish, and measured the water temperature and plankton to come up with the best solution. Kim was also determined to train his crew to use the fishing equipment and methods he was familiar with, to a degree that bordered on obsession."

The sea was not the only thing that Kim learned about. Kim Jae-chul once told the following story.

"Once I became the head of the Fishing Division, the female staff would often bring me red or blue sales statements, but I knew nothing about numbers because I had been trained as a captain. So I started attending a bookkeeping academy in the evenings to learn accounting."

If there was something that Kim didn't know, he would solve the problem with education, which led to his obsession with figures as a business leader later in life.

The Sorrow of Living in a Backwards Country

The unique experiences that Kim went through at Durban Port in South Africa as the head of the fleet stayed with him for a long time.

At the time, a Japanese marine firm called Toshoku had

berthed a 5,000 ton large refrigerated carrier at Tamatave Port in Madagascar. When tuna vessels entered the port, they would drop anchor nearby and unload their cargo in the order they arrived. Albacore was exported to the US to make canned tuna, while the tuna and bigeye tuna were sold to Japan to be used as raw fish, and the yellowfin and swordfish were mainly sent to Italy. In this way, the Japanese had established a firm position in Africa.

Due to the rudimentary communications facilities at that time, business was mostly conducted in hotels once a fleet called into port. Despite South Africa's strict apartheid policy, the Japanese received the same treatment as whites, while other people of color were treated as blacks. The hotels for blacks had no communications equipment, so Kim tried to gain entry to a hotel for whites but was denied.

He demanded the same treatment as the Japanese, tenaciously arguing his case. "If you keep acting like this, I'm going to take my ship elsewhere," he threatened. In the end, Kim was permitted to stay and conduct business in a hotel for whites.

"Korea is a much richer country now, so people no longer

have to deal with that kind of discrimination. But back then, the country was in a difficult situation, and I routinely faced discrimination when I traveled abroad."

In 1967, Korea Wonyang Fisheries owned more fleets than any other deep sea fishing company in Korea. They were all state-of-the-art 230-ton vessels, with five working in Samoa and eight deployed in the Indian Ocean. That same year, seven other ships were launched for the first time to explore fishing grounds for future operations.

This was an even better opportunity for Kim, as there not many people equipped with the hands-on knowledge to ensure the smooth operation of overseas projects.

As the company grew, Kim often went on business trips to Africa to make predictions about the market based on the fishing conditions and adjust the port entry schedule for ships. This afforded Kim with many opportunities to meet officials from the Japanese fishing industry.

At the time, there were no direct flights from Seoul to Africa. Korea was nothing but a poor backwater country in Asia that was mostly known for the Korean War. This led to an overwhelming sense of sorrow whenever Kim passed through immigration.

"The sense of grief I felt stayed with me for a long time. The things I experienced during that time had a large impact on me, driving me to start a business and propelling me forward in life to where I stand now. Although individualism is more prevalent these days, people from my generation always thought of our country first. Those dark memories roused me to action, and motivated me to help people by working hard on my business."

If this was the experience of Koreans on overseas business trips, one can only imagine what the life of ordinary sailors must have been like.

Many of the principles that Kim held dear as a businessman stem from his experiences as a youth, including viewing financial deficits as a sin, refusing to ask for help from the state and investing in staff. Kim's firm belief that his company, his family and even himself would not exist without his country is a positive legacy of his painful experiences as a young man who hailed from a backward country.

A Life Taught by the Sea

Kim Jae-chul is considered a 'legend' by the Korean community in Samoa these days. This is because Kim's vessel was the first Korean ship to sell tuna to StarKist, an American firm, and also because he later acquired that same company in 2008. Even now, Kim views Samoa as an important business stronghold and the hometown of his heart.

The beliefs that have influenced his life can be neatly summarized as the 'Eight Fundamentals of Life and Management.'

1) There is an absolute being that is beyond human control

"Although I am not religious, I have felt the infiniteness of the universe when I saw the countless stars in the night sky as I lived at sea, and felt the formidableness of nature as I fought with mountainous waves on stormy seas."

To Kim, the vast ocean is an absolute being that rules over everything on earth, and it taught him about the frailty of human existence.

2) You must have a clear view of life and death, and seek to live with integrity

"When a giant wave looms right before your eyes, everything from your past flashes through your mind. In that moment, I resolved to life a life without shame if I made it back alive. That is why I have always given my best, even if not everything worked out as I planned it."

The firm belief that one must not be left wanting in life was a gift that Kim received from the sea.

3) Being alive and able to work is a blessing

There are many fatal accidents at sea. Seeing the crewmates that you shared joys and sorrows with pass away right before your eyes gives people a completely different perspective on death. This taught Kim that although life is about striving to achieve, it can all be over in an instant.

When I asked Kim why he works, he gave the following reply. "It is only through work that self-actualization is possible and you can achieve your God-given purpose. Work is not something to be avoided, but a tool for achieving the purpose you were given when you were born into this world. It's a privilege. In a company, some people stop working once they get promoted and delegate everything to their subordinates. This is the opposite of personal development. In fact, that is precisely the moment that you stop developing."

4) There is little to brag about in this world

In the vast ocean, there is no such thing as a hierarchy. The ocean taught Kim about 'equality.' The fact that Kim treats 'keeping a low profile' and refraining from showing off as a revered part of his life is also due to a truth he learned from the sea. Kim has been able to avoid any troubles related to money, personal relationships or separation of public and private life because of the clear life principles he was taught at sea.

"Everyday troubles did not really faze me, and when other people were struggling, I found myself even more ready to take on a challenge. What in this world could be more frightening than death? When I remembered standing in a life or death situation, I was able to refresh my mind." In this sense, the ocean taught Kim to be humble.

5) Life itself is not different from war

Kim was quick to let go of any romantic notions and learn that life is a battle for survival. He learned at sea that a business can come crashing down in an instant.

"Even though they may be rough, sailors do not resort to petty tricks. The sea does not accept excuses or pull any punches. When you're out at sea, you will die if your skills are not up to scratch."

6) Those who fail to act will not receive any favors

Success is impossible without hard work. Although the same applies to catching the largest haul of fish, it is only possible to escape unscathed from a fierce storm by doing your damnedest to survive. Nothing can be achieved by waiting.

Survival and the laurels of success will only be granted to those who are always hustling and boldly take on challenges. Those who take the easy route and seek out calm waters to avoid danger will not be granted the opportunity to return with a full boat.

Kim's life principles are also reflected in his management

philosophy. He says that the rules of survival for a company are no different from those in life.

7) Nothing in this world is trivial

The same principles apply to any ship at sea, whether it weighs 100 tons or 200 tons. A small crack in the steel plating can spell disaster for the ship. Kim included 'paying close attention to small things' in his code of conduct for corporate management because he knows that failure to do so can have fatal consequences.

"No matter how large a ship may be, one small hole spells disaster. If the engine stops working during a storm because of a small defect in a component, everyone will die. It is crucial to pay close attention to details, no matter how small."

8) The power to motivate people comes from sacrifice and leading by example

The Jinam II, the first vessel that Kim worked on in the South Pacific, was an 80-ton ship of about 30 meters. The 18 crew members, including the captain, spent several months together in cramped conditions. As a young captain, Kim learned how to motivate his crew, even though many of them were old enough to be his father. He learned from experience that the best way to spur people to action was leading by example.

How to Become a Great Captain

Make Experiences and Knowledge Systematic

Kim Jae-chul adopted scientific methods to improve his abilities. The same applies to business, where he focused on figures over feelings and rejects conventional wisdom and preconceptions. He proved the effectiveness of the fishing methods he developed by testing them in the field. Kim spent his life fighting against preconceived ideas.

The Power of 'Field Notes'

Whatever the task, making a half-hearted effort will never lead to good results.

The method adopted by Kim is akin to the hypothetical deductive method used for scientific research. This method consists of four main stages.

① Clearly define the research target or problem. Whether all the branch lines tied to the main line are effective at catching tuna.

② Come up with a hypothesis that may solve the problem. Contrary to conventional wisdom, among the eight branch lines tied to the main line, the two at the very ends do not perform a useful function.

③ Make a prediction about what will occur if the hypothesis is correct. The hooks attached to the branch lines located at the far ends will not contribute to the catch because they do not perform a useful function.

④ Conduct the experiment, make observations and gather data, then adopt the hypothesis if it is correct and discard it if it is not.

Kim proved that his hypothesis was correct by keeping 'field notes.' He immediately implemented the change, and succeeded in taking his fishing methods to the next level.

Kim took advantage of his intellectual curiosity, passion for innovation, acute power of observation and scientific research methods to make continual improvements to his fishing methods. This is what enabled him to found Dongwon Group.

Kim's devotion to innovation can be seen in the fact that he often tells his executives "Don't become close friends with anyone who plans to live the second forty years of their life the same way they lived the first half."

The Traits of a First-rate Captain

Kim identifies four key traits a captain should possess, which contain broader truths that can be applied to everyday life.

① A captain that is skilled at catching fish anytime, anywhere Good captains have the skills to find the fish on their own.

② A captain that is close with other captains who are also skilled at catching fish Good captains can offset their weaknesses to some degree through their friends Those who are adept at building networks of personal connections can always receive help from competent people around them.

③ A captain that consistently seeks to find the fish despite being of only average ability Good captains are sincere, diligent and focused, and are able to get as close as possible to the goal in the first point, even if they cannot achieve it

④ A captain that is willing to leap to action after hearing nothing more than a rumor. Fishing vessels usually announce their catch and location three times per day. However, they tend to avoid saying anything when they have caught a lot.

Part II

The Path to Entrepreneurship

story 1

An Opportunity Earned through Reputation

The Fruits of a Life of Hard Work

In 1968, Kim Jae-chul resigned from his position and started preparing to found his own company. He was 34 at the time. The deep sea fishing industry is capital-intensive. Kim was the first former captain to start his own deep sea fishing company, which set off alarm bells for other business owners.

A Watchful Eye from Japanese Fishermen

Through the Tamatave Port in Madagascar, Kim had been responsible for trading his catch with foreign businessmen, and was able to handle the sale of marine products, taking on loans and the acquisition of vessels without making any errors.

People began to take note of his hard work, in particular the Japanese businessmen.

A Special Connection to Chairman Hagiwara

Kim Jae-chul's decision to head down the path towards entrepreneurship was at the recommendation of Hagiwara Nobuo, a Japanese CEO. Hagiwara was eight years older than Kim and the chairman of Dairen Reishyo. His business owned ten cargo ships that transported tuna to Japan for use in raw fish dishes.

Hagiwara had observed the unusual way in which Kim devoted himself to earning for his company, as if the business was his own. It was possible to commit fraud when purchasing supplies such as fishing gear, bait and food for the ship, but Kim always acted with integrity and made sure that the figures were accurate. Hagiwara was also well aware of Kim's reputation and how he handled his work at the company headquarters. He was certain that Kim would succeed as an entrepreneur, because he was not only an outstanding captain, but also well versed in the ins and outs of the fishing trade.

Although Kim was hesitant about starting his own business at such a young age because of the risk, meeting Hagiwara ended up becoming a major event in his life when he was ultimately persuaded to found his own company.

"If it weren't for you, I could control your company as I please," Hagiwara joked with Kim. "But since you drive a hard bargain, I have to be careful."

There is a story that offers insight into what Hagiwara thought of Kim. When Hagiwara was planning to hand the business down to his son, he sent him to live with Kim for a year so that he could learn about the trade at Dongwon Industries.

A Connection through a Connection Once Kim's company was established, Hagiwara told him "You are the kind of person who needs to make it big, and Toshoku and Dairen Reishyo are too small. You can't deal only with companies like us. I'm going to introduce you to Mitsubishi, so I hope you can start to do business them them."

Thanks to Hagiwara, Kim was able to secure a long business relationship with Mitsubishi, Japan's largest general trading firm.

Doing Business with Mitsubishi

Another important figure that Kim met around this time was Makihara Minoru, the CEO of Mitsubishi. Makihara first met Kim in the mid-1970s.

While serving as the deputy head of Mitsubishi's Fishing Division, he traveled to Korea for a ship owners meeting and had the opportunity to meet a number of people. His direct superior told him "You won't be able to recall the names and faces of all the Korean ship owners, but make sure you remember Kim Jae-chul." Thanks to the relationship between Dongwon and Mitsubishi, the two companies were able to provide a lot of assistance to each other as they grew. Even during the Asian Financial Crisis, Dongwon received a lot of help.

Makihara reflected on the situation at that time in an

article submitted to the Nikkei newspaper titled 'my resume.'

> I was very close to Korean ship owners as well. Kim was one of them. As intellectual as he was, he possessed a great talent as a ship owner and business executive. He wanted to go and study at Harvard Business School, and asked me to write a letter of recommendation for him. "That would take at least 13 weeks," I said. "Can you afford to be away from the office for that long?" He replied that the company would be fine since he could delegate authority to someone else, and that he planned to start studying English from now on. Impressed by Kim's passion for learning, I wrote him a letter of recommendation.

Dongwon Industries continued to experience steady growth under the leadership of Kim, and it was while taking an AMP course at Harvard that he came up with the idea to acquire Hanshin Securities, the predecessor to Korea Investment Holdings.

One feature that has been confirmed time and time again through the life of Kim Jae-chul is the importance of personal relationships based on trust.

His connection with Makihara transcends generations.

Kim Nam-goo, the vice president of Korea Investment Holdings, asked Makihara for a favor when he was seeking admission to Keio University's School of Business. Makihara later received a thank you letter from Professor Kobayashi at Keio University for "recommending such an outstanding student." Makihara once wrote "That was the first time I had received a letter of thanks after writing a recommendation."

When Kim's juniors sought advice from him on starting a business, he would say "In a capitalist society, credit is money. Don't become too focused on the money you can see; you need to pay even more attention to the credit you can't see. I was able to grow during times of crisis because of people who believed in me, and that is how I ended up where I am today."

Deep Sea Sailors and Miners and Nurses Sent to Germany

"The hardship you are currently enduring is a noble act of service and sacrifice that will leave something meaningful behind for your homeland and descendants."

This excerpt is taken from words of encouragement offered

by President Park Chung-hee in front of rows of deep sea sailors in September 1968. Park's wife, Yuk Yeong-su, had to dab at her eyes with a handkerchief on several occasions as she looked out from the podium at the rough, tanned exterior of the Korean sailors they were greeting in the middle of the South Pacific.

During the 1970s, not a penny of foreign currency was wasted. Across the country, Koreans were doing anything and everything they could to earn foreign currency. Between 1958 and 1979, the deep sea fishing industry recorded $2 billion in exports in total. This figure is 20 times the amount remitted to Korea by the 19,000 miners and nurses who were sent to work in Germany over a ten-year period. This hard-earned cash formed the foundations of Korea's development, and we must not forget that such an achievement did not materialize out of thin air.

At the same time, countless men lost their lives in seas far away from home while pioneering new fishing grounds. In total, 327 of those that perished are buried across eight locations, including 93 bodies recovered from Samoa, 118 from Las Palmas and 93 from Suriname. These deaths are lamentable.

Kim Jae-chul approached officials from the Korea Overseas Fisheries Association on several occasions to encourage the association to look after the overseas tombs of Korean sailors. As a result of this, overseas tombs for Korean sailors have been properly maintained since the completion of a government-funded project launched in 2002 to look after such burial grounds.

Seizing Opportunities

The history of development in the Korean deep sea fishing industry is closely related to two events. The first was the release of the Park Chung-hee administration's five-year economic plan, and the second was the decision by a Japanese general trading firm to loan secondhand ships to Korea as chartered vessels and provide support to cover operating expenses. The government's decision to offer payment guarantees or shipbuilding subsidies to private firms also served as a catalyst for growth in the industry.

The number of fishing vessels, which stood at five in 1962,

had grown to 65 by 1965 thanks to a loan of 30 ships from Italy and France. By 1969, when Kim handed in his letter of resignation, there was a total of 224 ships spread across 24 companies, including the Korea Maritime Development Service. President Park's visit to Samoa can be understood as part of his policy to foster exporters by offering encouragement to workers in a strategic export industry.

Japanese general trading firms also provided support of up to $200,000 per ship in the form of lines of credit. Because they had plenty of capital and control of the market, these firms were able to exert substantial influence on the price of tuna. At the time, most deep sea fishing companies sold to certain general trading firms in Japan, and Kim dealt with Mitsubishi, Mitsui and Itochu. The credit built up in this way made a large contribution to development in the industry.

A Meeting with Itochu CEO Ryuzo Sejima

When the topic of 'paying close attention to small and trivial details' came up, Kim mentioned the time he met Ryuzo Sejima, the CEO of Itochu. Ryuzo is the protagonist in Fumo Chitai, a book that has been widely read in Korea.

By picking up on the early signs of world events such as the Middle East War and Chinese invasion of Vietnam in 1967, and the oil shocks of 1973, Ryuzo was able to earn massive profits for his company. After reading Fumo Chitai at an early stage, Kim Jae-chul became determined to meet Ryuzo Sejima in person. Kim had learned to do whatever it took to create an opportunity to meet and learn from a person if he felt it was necessary.

Kim and Ryuzo began to exchange ideas about what was happening in the world in a restaurant in Japan. For the majority of the conversation, it was Kim asking questions and Ryuzo responding. Ryuzo talked about how he pulled strings behind the scenes while traveling back and forth between Korean, his relationship with Samsung founder Lee Byung-chul, and how he had advised Kim Jong-pil to create a Korean general trading company to support the country's economic growth.

As the two of them talked, Ryuzo took a liking to Kim as he was barraged with a torrent of questions. "After talking with you, it feels like I have been interrogated at a parliamentary hearing in the Korean National Assembly," he laughed. Kim asked Ryuzo how he could become better at predicting the future. Ryuzo responded by sharing his experience and wisdom.

"When people read the newspaper, they look at the longer three or five-paragraph stories. But you won't find any opportunities there. The opportunities lie in the small articles in the international section. If we take flowers as a metaphor, the five-paragraph articles are flowers that have already bloomed, while the one-paragraph stories are waiting to blossom. There aren't any opportunities in flowers that have already bloomed."

There are three points worth taking note of here. The first is that Kim resolved to go to Japan and meet Ryuzo in person after reading Fumo Chitai. He always took action when he believed there was something to be learned.

The second is that Kim always thoroughly prepared before meeting someone. He believed that by figuring out what he wished to learn in advance, he could obtain more information and knowledge in a short period of time.

The third is making a good impression on your

counterpart. Is there anyone who would not take a liking to someone who enthusiastically asks a lot of questions? Ryuzo was also 23 years older than Kim, and he opened his mind to him in their first meeting.

"Whenever I arrived at or left the office, I remember that Ryuzo would courteously walk me to the elevator to see me off," Kim recalled.

story 2

First Steps toward Founding a Company

Five Considerations before Founding a Company

With a keen awareness of the harsh competition in the business world, Kim Jae-chul always took five things into consideration when making a decision.

1) What do I currently have to work with?

Kim took stock of his hands-on experience as a captain, his general understanding of the deep sea fishing industry and the pool of human resources available to him.

2) What capital is available to me?

Although he didn't have any capital of his own, Kim owned ships that could be used as collateral and a reliable group of friends who could help him to cover expenses.

3) Do I know where I need to go?

Seeing the dominating position held by Japanese firms in the deep sea fishing industry helped Kim to develop clear goals and a concrete vision.

4) Do I have a good understanding of the field I aim to enter?

Kim had a deep understanding of the deep sea fishing business. This was one area in which he had a clear competitive edge over other ship owners.

5) Can I be certain about the future?

Kim paid close attention to the growing demand for marine products. He was certain that this was not a temporary trend, and that Japan would continue to experience rapid economic growth for a long period of time. In terms of changes in industry structure, he firmly believed that Korea could step up to replace the declining Japanese deep sea fishing industry.

The rise and fall of Japan presented Korea with some important lessons and a number of business opportunities. For example, Ho-Am Lee Byung-chul frequently visited Japan and worked hard to seek out business opportunities through Japan. The industrial structure of a country continues to change in line with the nation's stage of development, and companies that fail to adapt inevitably fall behind.

Even now, Kim voraciously reads the Nikkei newspaper. This is an important part of his efforts to predict the future.

The State of the Industry at the Time of Dongwon's Establishment

Although Kim could confidently answer the five questions above, the prospects looked grim for the Korean deep sea fishing industry at the time.

① Overfishing had led to a marked decline in hauls from the South Pacific

② The rapid growth in the number of deep sea vessels had led to excess supply.

③ In order to keep the growth of the rapidly expanding Korean deep sea fishing industry in check, the Japanese government had enacted a new law to regulate fishing by foreign nationals in 1967.

④ International regulations on resource conservation were expected to ramp up. In this sense, Kim was well aware that the tuna industry faced an uncertain future.

The Launch of Dongwon Industries

Nevertheless, Kim founded Dongwon Industries in April 1969. The company began with three employees in a small 46 square meter office.

What transpired in the deep sea fishing industry since 1968? Among the top 12 exporters at the time, not a single company run by the original founder or their next of kin still remains. Most of the leading companies today were latecomers to the industry.

Based on current standards, the only companies that have

grown to a certain size are Hansung Enterprise, Dongwon Industries, Daerim Fisheries, Oyang Corporation and Dong Won Fisheries, and as of 2013, only two companies own more than 20 ships. Dongwon Industries has 41 vessels, while Sajo Industries owns 42.

Although there were only 24 firms in the industry back in 1969 when Kim founded Dongwon Industries, this figure peaked at 212 firms in 1992, which owned a total of 810 ships between them. The industry experienced rapid decline since that point, with only 75 companies remaining in 2013.

A Business Built on Credit

Kim Jae-chul was 34 years old when he founded his own company. He signed a contract for a loan of $370,000 from Olympia Trading, the US branch of the Japanese firm Toshoku, for the Dongwon XXXI and XXXIII. It appeared that Hagiwara had lent Kim a line of credit as collateral.

The Success of the First Ship, the Dongwon XXXI

There were two notable features of the Dongwon XXXI,

the first vessel acquired by Kim in 1969.

The first is that it was huge by standards at that time, weighing in at 481 tons. The reason that Kim's actions are synonymous with the history of Korea's deep sea fishing industry is that he always sought to get ahead of the rest. He was ahead of the times when it came to upgrading the size of independent tuna fishing vessels.

The ship was also a mother ship that carried a supporting longline vessel on board, the first time this technique had been adopted in Korea.

The Strength of an Entrepreneur with Hands-on Experience

The new mother ship fishing technique that Kim had discovered through his on-board experience and research exceeded expectations on its maiden voyage. The skipper of the vessel, Captain Lee Jung-gi, recounted the following story.

"Although we were a single ship, in reality we could perform the work of two vessels. Because we had loaded a 20-ton support vessel on board a 500-ton mother ship, we could effectively carry the haul of two boats. It only took us 24 hours to travel the distance that other ships would take 27 hours to cover. This was only possible with an experienced captain who was capable of making quick decisions.

Kim had hoped that the Dongwon XXXI could operate 230 days a year, with an average daily catch of 2.5 tons, an annual haul of 575 tons, and annual revenue of $170,000.

However, 25 months later, the ship had already brought in 2,500 tons and $750,000 in revenue. Kim even received a presidential commendation that year for his contribution to earning foreign currency. From that point on, the Dongwon XXXI continued to achieve great success, bringing in a full haul every four months on average and setting a new record for itself on six occasions.

story 3

Establishing the Business Foundations

A Continued Commitment to Challenge and Transformation

In the initial stages, the process through which Kim Jae-chul laid a foundation for his business represented a historic expansion in fishing grounds. This was accompanied by efforts to increase hauls through the application of newly developed fishing techniques.

With the Dongwon XXXI as an anchor, Dongwon Industries developed into a leading company with a fleet of tuna vessels that was the envy of the world. Of course, Dongwon lived through the first and second rounds of oil shocks, and also faced a crisis when the Soviet Union and United States expanded their marine territories by 200 nautical miles, but the company was able to adeptly overcome these challenges.

Innovation through New Fishing Techniques

Kim was well aware that his flourishing business could fall into crisis at any time, and continued to seek out new possibilities. He was also skilled at finding a new perspective on conventional wisdom. Even with the Dongwon XXXI, Kim's secret to success lay in making the right moves at the right time, such as developing the mother ship technique, reanalyzing existing fishing grounds and hiring top quality captains and crews.

This innovation spurred development across the entire deep sea fishing industry. Kim also achieved innovation in tuna longlining, squid pole fishing and bonito pole fishing.

Jumping into Squid Pole Fishing

Even while establishing a foundation for his business through tuna longlining, Kim continued to conduct research on new fishing grounds, techniques and equipment. One of his greatest early successes was the development of squid pole fishing, or jigging.

This technique was first implemented in 1971, and is significant for five reasons.

① It was the first time a 300-ton tuna longlining vessel had been remodeled to perform squid pole fishing in Sakhalin waters.

② The experience gained from this endeavor was of great benefit to the deep sea squid pole fishing industry.

③ The success of squid pole fishing gave Kim the confidence to try bonito pole fishing in waters near Ghana in 1973.

④ It also gave him the confidence to try trawl fishing in the northern seas.

⑤ As the first new line of business developed in the marine industry, squid pole fishing helped to diversify the industry.

Putting the Right Man in the Right Place

"The greatest enemy of knowledge is not ignorance, but thinking that you know the answer." In other words, boldly hiring new blood is the key to success for a new project. The men that Kim hired to pioneer his new fishing techniques were not older fishermen with a wealth of experience. Instead, he chose an ambitious captain in his late 20s that had only recently joined the company after working on deep sea vessels for five years. The bold decision to appoint a young captain who was capable of thinking outside the box was impressive.

When he proposed the project to the young man, Kim said "How would you like to head out from the east coast and give squid pole fishing a try?" As soon as he heard the reply "I will do my best," Kim issued the following command. "Great, then start by remodeling the Dongwon XXXV into a squid pole fishing ship."

During the first voyage, which lasted a month and a half, the Dongwon XXXV hauled in a catch of 15,300 boxes, earning $90,000. This was a grand achievement that made up for the misfortune the Dongwon XXXV had suffered in the Indian Ocean.

Pioneering New Fishing Grounds with Bonito Pole Fishing

When Kim tried out bonito pole fishing from the Tema base in Ghana in 1972, it was the first time a Korean company had succeeded in commercializing the technique.

This method involves throwing live anchovies into the water as bait once a school of tuna has been detected, then hauling the tuna in with poles. At the time, it was a highly difficult technique to perform.

Once Kim identified the technique's potential, he took two steps to overcome these technical difficulties. First, he sent Kim Yong-mun, who had been successful at squid pole fishing, to Ghana to study the technique. Second, he signed a training contract with the US canned tuna firm StarKist so that his crews could learn the new technique of pole fishing.

Based on this foundation, the Dongwon DCCCI was remodeled into a bonito pole fishing vessel after being acquired from Japan, and entered Ghanaian waters in 1973. The Dongwon DCCCI performed above expectations, and the Dongwon DCCCIII, DCCCVI and DCCCVII also enjoyed great success in the endeavor before the project was finally scrapped in 1978. Bonita pole fishing led to the advent of new fishing grounds for the deep sea industry over the following decade.

However, everything changes. Rising oil prices and the declaration that expanded marine territories by 200 nautical miles caused the pole fishing industry to experience decline from 1979, and the technique was eventually made obsolete by the advent of purse seine fishing in 1980.

At this point, I would like to make a hypothesis that applies to every industry. This is a kind of 'golden rule' for business success. Kim Jae-chul is one man who has faithfully adhered to this rule. The rule is that when a certain line of business becomes highly profitable, entrepreneurs must seek out another source of growth.

First Steps into the Sablefish Industry

Kim continued to seek out new fishing grounds across the South Pacific, Indian and Atlantic oceans, and also began engaging in longlining and deep sea trawling for sablefish in the northern seas. Trawl fishing refers to a technique where a power lathe drags in a sack-shaped net filled with fish.

When the price of fish fell due to an excess supply of

pollack from the northern seas, catching sablefish was the solution. Lowering hooks down to near the ocean floor to catch fish that dwelled in the depths proved to be a success when it was tried for the first time. Sablefish were in great demand and sold for a high price, which led to renewed promise for northern sea fishing that had previously been heavily weighted towards pollack.

Sablefish trawling experienced a boom from 1977 up until the US expanded its economic zone by 200 nautical miles, but after the US imposed a quota of 3,800 tons on sablefish, only seven ships remained in the North Pacific while the rest dispersed to waters near New Zealand or Mexico. By the time the quota allocation was removed in 1984, there was already no place left for sablefish trawling.

Trying out Midwater Trawl Nets

On September 25, 1979, the Dong-a Ilbo ran a special story titled 'Sailors Fleeing from Regulation.'

This article analyzed the crisis facing the deep sea fishing industry and cited reasons for the gap between Korea and more advanced countries. The reasons listed were a failure to adopt midwater trawling and enter the purse seine fishing business. However, Kim was ultimately able to resolve both of these problems by taking on new challenges.

The first Korean ship to successfully employ midwater trawling was the 1,860-ton Yuyang, owned by Dongwon Industries, in 1978. Trawling is also called 'sniping' because it involves dragging a large sack-shaped net towards the area where fish are located. Although bottom trawling was developed first, the presence of obstacles on the sea floor often caused damage to fishing equipment, which made midwater trawling a more attractive proposition.

Kim's answer to the question "How can we be the first to introduce midwater trawling?" was simple. It all began from the idea of catching pollack when they rose to the surface, even though the fish were bottom dwellers.

Prior to the extension of the economic zone, trawlers in the northern seas could fish in waters as close as 12 miles from the US or Soviet Union coast. These coastal waters were 200-300 meters deep and featured a continental shelf with a gradual incline, leading to greater hauls of fish. However, everything turned on its head when the Yuyang entered the northern seas. The open waters outside the 200 nautical mile radius were 4,000-5,000 meters deep. Up until that point, no Korean fishing vessels had used midwater trawling.

When the Yuyang successfully performed a test operation after lengthy research, Kim used midwater nets on the Sinyang as well, a 2,000-ton ship that was acquired the following year. After leaving port in March 1979, the ship brought in 5,100 tons of pollack over a five-month voyage. Four thousand tons of the haul were transferred to a cargo ship, while the remaining 1,100 tons were brought home. Upon seeing this, other companies also began to use upgraded fishing equipment from 1979.

Improvements to Trawling Equipment

Kim Jae-chul also achieved innovation through the Dongsan, a 4,500-ton factory mother ship equipped with upgraded trawling equipment.

Up until that point, no one had doubted the conventional wisdom that the size of the mesh in nets should correlate with the size of the fish. It seemed only natural that ships of all sizes should use the same size mesh. However, after conducting an investigation in Japan, Kim learned how frightening preconceptions can be.

Korea was using nets with a mesh of 1m, while Japanese boats used nets of 4m mesh. Rather than being inclined to escape through the large holes in the net, fish were dazzled by the glimmering mesh and tended to congregate near the center.

The fact that 4,000 ton Korean trawlers were using the same nets as 340 ton Japanese trawlers demonstrated that Korean ships were subject to far greater water resistance from using nets with smaller mesh. Kim decided to make nets with a 5m mesh. This allowed the nets to cover a greater area and catch more fish, while also reducing water resistance.

Exploring New Fishing Grounds

"Aren't there any other fishing grounds?" This is the question Kim Jae-chul continued to pose throughout his life. While the introduction of new fishing techniques led to qualitative progress in Kim's business, it was the discovery of new fishing grounds that led to quantitative upgrades. This is because a company must expand its business portfolio in order to achieve continued growth.

Another notable expansion in fishing grounds took place in 1973. The Dongwon DCCCI, which had led the adoption of bonito pole fishing using Tema Port in Ghana as a base, started to make inroads into fishing grounds in the Atlantic Ocean.

After establishing a base in Las Palmas in 1974, three trawlers managed to reel in 19,000 tons of fish, which served as a cornerstone for the company's growth. At the time, there were 64 Korean trawlers fishing in the Atlantic, but this number had already grown to 112 by 1975.

Developing Fishing Grounds in Indonesia

At the beginning of the 1990s, many vessels were fishing in grounds near Indonesia. Up to 75% of trawlers in the South Pacific were fishing in Indonesian waters, which helped to prop up growth in the Korean deep sea fishing industry.

After the Dongwon CI proved the commercial viability of catching premium fish such as croaker, shrimp and cuttlefish near Indonesia during a test operation in 1987, Korean trawlers headed to the area en masse.

The Wings of Rapid Growth

By the 10th anniversary of Dongwon Industries, the company owned 22 large trawlers including the Dongsan, and revenue had grown from 41.29 million KRW (in 1969) to 15.758 billion KRW in 1979, a staggering annual growth rate of 81.3%.

By 1981, the company owned 25 ships. Among the newly obtained ships, the tuna purse seine ships Costa de Marfil and the Captain Kim are worthy of attention, as they represented the springboard for a new era of growth at Dongwon Industries.

The Eight Keys to Rapid Growth in the Early Stages

① With many years of hands-on experience in deep sea fishing, Kim Jae-chul had an edge over others who relied on capital to jump into the business.

② By hiring competent crews and putting the right man in the right place, Kim was successfully able to increase his hauls.

③ He had a relationship with a Japanese buyer that

was built on trust, and was able to grow his fleet by trading with Japanese companies that insisted on cash transactions. In other words, acquiring more ships led to greater revenue, which in turn enabled Kim to purchase more ships, creating a virtuous cycle.

④ Kim's fluency in Japanese enabled him to establish a professional network and take advantage of business opportunities.

⑤ He made sensible decisions in critical moments. Rather than follow the masses, Kim trusted his own judgment and insights to get ahead of the pack.

⑥ Kim's human attributes also played a large part in his success, in particular his upright values, ability to take action and dedication to empiricism.

By fulfilling his corporate duty of giving back to society by generating value, he helped to offset the damage caused to society by the many deep sea fishing companies that went bankrupt.

⑦ Staying focused was an important part of his mindset. Kim had a no-nonsense approach to life and did not waste his time on pointless activities.

⑧ He lived as if he was always fighting with his back to the wall and could help no one but himself. Kim believed that his ability was all that could save him, and stuck to this principle to the very end.

Kim Jae-chul's Keys to Success

Kim believes that the fundamental elements for success are repeatedly teaching people to adhere strictly to the principles, paying close attention to small details and boldly trying new things along with luck.

Kim reflected on the time his ships were captured as an example of overcoming adversity.

In 1979, 44 Korean trawlers fishing in the Atlantic Ocean were detained for intruding upon territorial waters, including three vessels owned by Dongwon. At the time, the ships and sailors could be set free if someone came forward to provide a financial guarantee.

It was Mitsubishi that stepped up to provide the guarantee, leading to the release of the detained ships and men. The captain of the Dongwon LXXXIII recounted the following about the dire situation they found themselves in.

"A week before returning to Korea, our ship was captured and detained in Agadir Port in Morocco for 100 days. At that time, Mitsubishi Corporation extended a helping hand to us."

A Bold Challenge with the Dongsan, a Factory Ship

Staking the Future of the Company on the Dongsan

In 1975, Kim Jae-chul commissioned a Japanese shipyard to build a 4,500 ton factory ship. This ship was a large vessel that could accommodate 150 people, and was equipped with a factory for processing fish. The ship caught pollack by dragging large sack-shaped nets through the water.

The Dongsan was capable of processing 200 tons of pollack per day, with crew members working in three shifts. When the ship left port, it would remain in the northern sea fishing grounds for ten months at a time, unloading its haul to cargo ships 4-5 times every two months. In the face of high oil prices, Kim had decided to embark on this alternate endeavor because he believed there was no future for labor-intensive fishing methods.

The sudden influx of pollack into the Korean market caused the price to plummet, which dealt a severe financial blow to fishermen who operated in coastal waters. In response to this, the government encouraged firms to begin exporting processed pollack.

Ships of All Sizes only Have a Single Captain

Spending $12.54 million to build a ship (at a time when Korea's per capita income was only $400) only four years after the business had been founded was a massive risk. For the same price, Kim could have built ten regular tuna longliners. Mitsubishi provided financial support for the project. At the time, Kim only owned 12 ships in total.

"My experience up until that point had shown me that every ship only needed a single captain, whether it was 100 tons or 5,000 tons." In terms of efficiency, Kim was certain that building larger ships was the better choice.

Securing Regular Clients

Kim's confidence that he would be able to obtain regular clients also played a part in his decision.

At the time, Mitsubishi had a factory for processing marine products in Masan which processed pollack for export to the US. The company agreed to be supplied by Korean firms. However, the rising price of pollack in Korea was an unexpected problem that threw a spanner in the works. In response to this, Kim came up with the idea of building a factory mother ship.

He sought to convince Mitsubishi that the ship he sought to build would be able to provide a steady supply of pollack to the factory. Mitsubishi was confident that Kim was the man who could meet their needs, but they were concerned that the investment was too large for the size of the company at the time.

Buoyed by the conviction that the project would be a success, Kim set about persuading Mitsubishi. Because the cost of labor in Korea was far cheaper than in Japan, and there was greater demand for pollack in Korea than in Japan, Kim was certain that there would be a market for the fish. Since he was staking the future of his company by making a massive investment in the Dongsan, he promised that he would work on board the ship himself to exercise direct control over operations.

Mitsubishi was ultimately swayed by his sincerity and agreed to help finance the project. On credit alone, and without any guarantee from the Korean government or a bank, Kim signed a contract to pay five installments over two years.

A Successful Decision

With 138 crew members on board, including 10 Japanese technicians, the Dongsan headed to the North Pacific on a historic expedition under the leadership of Kim Jae-chul. After only a month of fishing in waters near Kamchatka, the ship had already hauled in 3,000 tons of pollack. This feat was recorded by Cho Gap-je, a journalist from the Kookje Shinmun.

Despite the difficult conditions, Kim kept his promise of repaying Mitsubishi for the cost of the ship without missing a payment by even a single day. This became a hot topic in the fishing industries of both Korea and Japan.

He repeatedly stressed the fact that "the Dongsan played a pivotal role in the growth of Dongwon Industries." As a single vessel, the Dongsan often brought in a larger haul than all the ships in other fleets combined.

In terms of ship numbers and catch volume, the northern seas trawling business served as a pillar of the Korean deep sea trawling industry. The industry provided high quality protein to the Korean people, while also bolstering foreign currency earnings through the export of pollack that was processed both on land and at sea.

Staking the Future of the Company on Tuna Purse Seining

With assistance from Van Camp's of US, Jedong Industries invested a large sum of money in the tuna purse seining industry in 1971 but failed to achieve much success. In 1978, the Korea Marine Development Service and Jedong Industries launched Korea Purse Seine Fisheries as a joint venture, but this project also failed to bear fruit. Around this time, Jae-chul was the first to try tuna purse seine fishing from a helicopter.

As the most advanced technique, purse seine fishing required large-scale investment, cutting-edge technology and a highly trained workforce, which made it a risky investment for private companies. However, purse seining was Kim's ultimate goal and also what he dreamed of. 'Thirty Years of History in the Korean Deep Fishing Industry' contains the following description of how Korea was able to successfully adopt the purse seine method, when it taken more than 20 years to master the technique in Japan.

The purse seining technique involves loading 3-5 small boats and detector helicopters onto large mother ships. When a school of tuna appears, the small boats are set afloat to haul in the fish with nets.

Tuna longliners can carry 25 men and catch between 300 and 450 tons per year, while purse seiners can catch 12,000-15,000 tons with the same human resources investment. Nothing beats the purse seine technique, which makes it the ultimate fishing method.

Stories from the Deck of a Purse Seiner

"Skiff standby! Skiff standby! Skiff let go!"

When the captain gives the order, the skiff hanging from the side of the mother ship slide down into the water, and a fierce battle ensues between the tuna and the crew. The sight of a purse seiner catching fish resembles a warzone.

The helicopter dances above the water in pursuit of the school, while the mother ship charges ahead at full steam. When it is time to cast the nets after the furious chase, the captain stands atop the lookout tower and shouts "Skiff standby! Skiff standby" through a microphone, before giving the final order "Skiff let go!"

The small speedboat grab the ends of the 1,500 meter net and race around the perimeter of a circle atop the sea, while the mother ship expends an output of almost 5,000 horsepower to steam ahead in the opposite direction to form a complete circle and box in the fish.

To prevent the tuna from escaping, the speed boats also throw rounds of explosives into the water while reaching speeds of up to 60 knots. With the symphony created by the sounds of the dynamite exploding from the mother ship to prevent the tuna from escaping, the loud hammers banging on the ship's steel playing and the updates on the fish detector blasting out once a minute, the entire scene is chaotic. The innate herd instinct of tuna means that they will all disperse in an instant if even one fish flees from the net.

In addition to fish detectors, radars and satellite communications equipment, purse seiners also carry helicopters to track the movement of fish. There are also 3-7 skiff boats, net boats and speedboats that are used for catching fish.

There is a clear difference between longliners and purse seiners in terms of productivity. While independent fishing vessels catch an average of two tons per day, purse seiners bring in 18 tons. The gap is even greater in terms of annual volume, with average hauls of 430 tons and 4,500 tons respectively, and profit rates of 11.6% for tuna longliners and 21.8% for purse seiners.

Despite these large differences, purse seining requires a large capital investment and heavy training, so it is risky for a private enterprise to venture into the industry.

The cost of an 800-ton helicopter-loading purse seiner designed in the US and produced in France is $3.2 million, the equivalent of seven 300-ton independent fishing vessels.

However, the Costa de Marfil failed to live up to expectations in the initial stages. There were difficulties learning the technology and running the ship with a crew consisting of Spanish sailors.

When the Costa de Marfil returned to Busan Port after its maiden voyage of one year and three months, the accumulated losses already amounted to $2.8 million. Kim Jae-chul made sweeping changes to the direction of the project in order to rectify the situation. He gave up on the fishing grounds in the East Pacific and recruited a talented Japanese fisherman, then switched the equipment and fishing gear to better suit the conditions in the West Pacific.

In September 1980, he replaced the foreign sailors with a Korean crew and sent the ship to sea. On this occasion, Kim joined the crew on board the ship. This was partly to ensure the crew's safety and send a clear message to his client. However, the fish-detecting helicopter crashed in an accident while conducting a maneuver, and two years and three months after beginning operations, the accumulated losses had grown to $3.2 million.

The situation looked grim to the extent that rumors about the downfall of Dongwon began circulating within the industry. Nevertheless, Kim continued to believe that things would turn around if he could improve the proficiency of the on-board crew.

Purse Seining is Worth a Shot

Kim's experience on the ship confirmed the fact the problem lay with the crew's level of training rather than purse seining itself. Certain that the project would succeed, he quickly moved to occupy the fishing grounds.

While the Costa de Marfil was fishing in the West Pacific, Kim purchased a second, 1,500-ton French-built purse seiner called the Captain Kim. With the addition of the Giant Kim in 1982 and the World Kim in 1984, the company's fleet of purse seiners grew to four vessels.

Clever and Hardworking Koreans

In a situation where advanced fishing nations were reluctant to share their secrets, Koreans were able to unleash their sharp eyes, work ethic and ability to quickly learn new skills in the tuna purse seining industry.

At first, there were many helicopter accidents, and some were skeptical about the cost-effectiveness of the business. However, after hiring foreign pilots on high salaries, the introduction of helicopters served to greatly broaden the range of areas in which fish could be detected.

At the time, Dongwon Industries employed the largest number of pilots in Korea after Korean Air and Asiana Airlines. Korea's tuna purse seining industry later developed into an industry leader.

Although the Japanese had a long history of catching tuna, their vessels were not equipped with helicopter facilities, and only a limited number of ships from Taiwan and the US carried helicopters. In contrast, Korea carried helicopters on large ships right from the outset.

By boldly venturing into the tuna purse seining business, Kim had set the standards that would remain in place in the industry for decades. This not only helped to push Korea into the leading group of purse seining nations, but also made the country a leader in innovation.

Greater Efficiency through Refrigerated Cargo Ships

As recently as the early 1980s, US tuna purse seiners did not have any refrigerated cargo ships. They had to return to port to unload their haul, and the ships that arrived first had no choice but to remained moored in the port for 30-60 days until unloading was complete.

At this time, Kim introduced the so-called 'two-way' method where refrigerated cargo ships would carry food, oil and other articles to ships working at sea before being loaded with fish and returning to port. This method greatly improved the efficiency of fishing operations, and played a pivotal role in helping Korea gain a foothold in the early stages of the purse seining industry.

Innovation in Fishing Equipment Using the Nature of Tuna

When Kim first entered the purse seining business, Spanish and US vessels were hauling in 2,000 tons a year, but the development of new equipment raised this figure to between 5,000 and 6,000 tons, with current hauls reaching as high as 10,000 tons. One vessel recently recorded a haul of 15,000 tons. In this respect, Kim played an important role in boosting hauls through innovation in fishing equipment.

The Courage to Stand Strong in Adverse Circumstances

"Tuna purse seiners made a large contribution to Dongwon Group's expansion." After Kim entered the tune purse seining business in 1980, Sajo Industries entered the fray in 1987, followed by Silla Deep Sea Fisheries in 1990. By 1992, there were 11 firms in the industry, but nowadays only Dongwon Industries, Sajo Industries, Silla Deep Sea Fisheries and Hansung Enterprise remain, with the rest making an inglorious exit from the stage.

As of 2013, purse seining accounted for 44% of the deep sea fishing industry, or 240,000 of the 550,000 tons of fish caught in Korea. The scope of fishing areas has also expanded to include waters in the West Pacific near Kiribati, Tuvalu, Papua New Guinea, Micronesia, the Marshall Islands, Nauru and the Solomon Islands. This was the result of new fishing grounds discovered by Korea.

As of 2012, global tuna production stood at 4.55 million tons, with 2.64 million tons or 58% caught in the Midwest Pacific. There are five factors were noting here.

① Fifteen percent of the haul from the mid-Pacific was caught by Korean tuna purse seiners, although they accounted for only 6% of all vessels (28 in total).

② While average productivity per ship was 1,000 tons in the early 1980s, the figure has stood at 8,000 tons since 2006.

③ Among Korean vessels, average productivity per ship was 2,000 tons in 1981, but grew to reach 260,000 tons in 2012.

④ After the first Korean purse seiner was launched in 1979, the number of vessels peaked at 39 in 1990.

⑤ Kim Jae-chul's achievements in the tuna purse seining industry have been recognized by the Korean government, and he was the first individual from the marine industry to be awarded the Bronze Order of Industrial Service Merit.

Dongwon Industries had the largest global fleet of tuna purse seiners in 2015 with 19 vessels, becoming the world's number one marine company when other types of ships are included.

Pioneering Multipurpose Tuna Purse Seiners

Multipurpose Tuna Purse Seiners and Traditional Tuna Purse Seiners

The first multipurpose tuna purse seiner was the 'Ocean Ace,' which left port in 2006. This was a 2,200-ton vessel with an average annual catch of 12,000 tons, of which 10,000 tons were used for canned tuna and the remainder was stored in deep freezers to be used as raw fish. The tuna stored in the freezers fetched 2.5 times the price of tuna used in cans. Compared to the 8,000 ton average annual haul of existing tuna purse seiners, the multipurpose ships could reach 13,000 tons per year. This also led to great innovation in terms of productivity.

Attempts to Overcome Conventional Wisdom

After being initially launched in 2006, Dongwon Industries' Ocean Ace was relaunched in 2014 as the Miraero. In 2010, the Korea Overseas Fisheries Association and Korea Multi-Purpose Accelerator Complex (KOMAC) began work on a project to design standards for multipurpose purse seiners, which concluded in 2011.

From this point on, companies such as Sajo Industries, Silla Deep Sea Fisheries and Hansung Enterprise began to build multipurpose tuna purse seiners in Korea. This led Korean purse seiners to gain a dominant edge in the competition.

Dongwon Industries currently owns seven multipurpose tuna purse seiners, including the Ocean Ace (2006), the Blue Ocean (2008), the Jang Bogo (2008), the Miraero (2014) and the Segyero (2014), with the Teraaka added alongside another vessel in 2015. Three of the company's twelve purse seiners were also remodeled into multipurpose vessels. With this move, Dongwon now has a total of 22 ships including ten multipurpose tuna purse seiners and 12 regular tuna purse seiners.

Overcoming Crises

Kim Jae-chul faced three major crises in the early stages of his business. The first round of oil shocks, the declaration that extended economic territory by 200 nautical miles and the second round of oil shocks.

Impact of the 1973 Oil Shocks

During the first oil shocks of 1973, international oil prices skyrocketed from $2.60 per barrel to $11.70 by December, and had increased sevenfold by the mid-1970s. When the APEC nations began reducing oil production, it caused a state of panic in countries that imported oil.

The large economic contraction that ensued in advanced countries cause demand for production to plummet, sending prices into a downward spiral. As a result of this, only 23 of the 62 ships fishing in the northern sea fishing grounds remained by the end of the year. However, up until the repercussions of the oil shocks started to be felt in 1974, Dongwon Industries was able to breeze through the crisis with Kim's substantial hauls from the Indian Ocean.

In the first year of the oil shocks, Dongwon posted year on year growth of 96.5%, which was more than enough to offset the spike in costs from rising oil prices. Even as the aftermath of the oil shocks continued to reverberate in 1976, Dongwon's fleet recorded year on year growth of 76-96% in the Atlantic, Pacific and North Pacific.

Ripples from the 200 Nautical Mile Extension to Economic Territory

Kim was soon faced with another crisis when the US and Soviet Union announced that they were extending their economic territory by 200 nautical miles.

Before the declaration, ships could fish in waters as close as 12 miles from the coast. But the greatly expanded economic territory was a disaster for the fishing industry, which lost half of its fishing grounds overnight.

At the time, the Dongsan was exploring fishing grounds in waters near New Zealand, and was able to bring in substantial hauls by spending 3-4 months in the northern seas and the rest of the near around New Zealand. However, falling fish prices and a 200 nautical mile extension to New Zealand's economic territory meant that the company had to look elsewhere for a breakthrough.

When this was followed by a sudden hike in the charges for fishing in waters near the coast of Africa, Dongwon decided to shut down its Las Palmas base. Nevertheless, the company was able to avoid bearing the brunt of financial damage because Kim had diversified Dongwon's business portfolio instead of relying on a single location.

A Shining Entrepreneurial Spirit after Losing the Northern Sea Fishing Grounds

Only five months after losing access to the fishing grounds in the northern seas, Dongwon fleets arrived in waters near New Zealand, Mexico, Iran and French Guiana. When I looked at the records of fishing ground exploration, I couldn't help but marvel at the entrepreneurial brilliance. It made me think of the saying "Those that desperately search will never die."

The Path of the Dongsan after Losing the Northern Sea Fishing Grounds

The Dongsan faced a perilous situation after being forced out of the northern seas, but departed for fishing grounds near New Zealand in 1977 after seeking out new possibilities. In the first year, the vessel returned with a full haul that sold for $2 million, but this was only enough to last 17 months. When New Zealand declared that it would also expand the country's economic territory by 200 nautical miles, the Dongsan was allocated a quota and ultimately returned to Busan Port in September 1978.

The ship was redeployed to engage in quota fishing in the northern seas in January 1979. The Dongsan would meet its quota in US territory before heading out to the open seas to fill the rest of the ship. It was only a tiny section of international waters, but the ship was able to haul in 1.5 to 2 million tons. Although the fishing ground was outside the jurisdiction of coastal states, accessing the location required passing through waters inside US economic territory, so ships had to be careful. Even so, the Dongsan was able to stay in business because of this location. Nevertheless, Kim Jae-chul continued to try everything he could to secure new fishing grounds.

He purchased the quota that had been allocated to a Vietnamese firm by the Soviet Union, which allowed Dongwon to conduct joint fishing with the Soviet Union in the Sea of Okhotsk. This was the first time a Korean vessel had been allowed in these waters since the 200 nautical mile declaration, and it came 12 years after leaving behind the rich fishing grounds in the northern seas.

This arrangement continued until 2003. The captain of the Dongsan recounted the following experience of visiting the Soviet Union, a nation with which Korea did not have formal diplomatic relations. "At the time, I received anticommunist education before entering the Soviet Union. While I was there, I received a Korean textbook for Russians, and was surprised to find that it contained the 'Beyond the Waves' on-board diary entry written by Kim Jae-chul in 1967. The Dongsan's entry into Soviet waters was the catalyst for more Korean businessmen visiting the Soviet Union, creating a cooperative relationship that contributed to the establishment of diplomatic relations between the two nations in 1990.

This is the background to the Dongsan being permitted to fish in the Sea of Okhotsk. Kim heard that the Vietnamese Vice Minister of Maritime Affairs wished to meet with him. At the time, Vietnam did not have diplomatic relations with South Korea. At the time, the Soviet Union allocated pollack quotas in the northern seas to satellite states such as Vietnam.

Upon meeting with Kim in Tokyo, the vice minister said "We cannot fill the quota given to us by the Soviet Union, so we hope that you can work with us as part of a joint venture."

When Kim replied "Korea does not have diplomatic relations with Vietnam or the Soviet Union, so how can Korean ships enter Soviet waters?" the vice minister told him that it would be no problem. "The Dongsan can enter Soviet waters if you hire a few Vietnamese crew members and fly a Vietnamese flag," he said. Kim thought to himself that these men had good heads on their shoulders.

This led to a three-way meeting between Korea, Vietnam and the Soviet Union in Saigon. However, the Soviet bureaucrats who had grown up in a communist system had no understanding of the concept of service, so communication was difficult and the negotiations broke down several times.

For instance, when a Soviet official suggested that the price of pollack should be the same in both Vietnam and the Soviet Union, Kim countered by pointing out this was impossible due to the cost of transporting the fish to Vietnam. In response, the Soviet official said "What kind of freight charge is there if we use a government vessel?" It must have been very difficult to negotiate with such people.

Kim heard an interesting story from the Vietnamese vice

minister at the time. “Our Soviet friends don't use their brains,” he said. Surprised at this statement, Kim said “Aren’t you living under a communist regime too?” Without missing a beat, the vice minister replied “We have only been living under such a regime for seven years, but it has been several decades for them in the Soviet Union, so their minds have completely rotted. I feel frustrated too.” The pair looked at each other and burst into laughter.

Around this time, Kim was asked to give a lecture at the Vietnamese Ministry of Maritime Affairs. When Kim replied that it would be difficult because of his schedule, the ministry adjusted their schedule for him and gathered all their staff at 10:30 in the evening to hear him speak. Kim recalls that he felt a sense of premonition that a brighter future lay in store for Vietnam.

The Dongsan left Busan Port in May 2003, and arrived in the Antarctic Ocean 50 days later. The ship caught krill between March and July, then fished in waters managed by fisheries in the South Pacific from July to November. In this area, the Dongsan caught horse mackerel and mackerel. After November, the ship sailed south to catch smelt in the icy waters until February, when krill fishing began once again. The haul was usually loaded onto cargo ships every 15 days and transported back to Busan Port.

In addition to catching krill in the Antarctic Ocean, in 2010 the Dongsan also successfully caught high-priced fish including southern fat bass and splendid alfonsino in waters managed by fisheries in the Southeast Pacific, a section of the ocean located to the east of Africa. The Dongsan's discovery of these new fishing grounds led to great expectations for catching expensive breeds of fish and the potential for exports.

After traversing the globe in search of new fishing grounds, the Dongsan was unfortunately retired in 2011 after suffering from a fire while moored in the Port of Cape Town. The changes in the fishing environment that affected the Dongsan are the same issues that the Korean deep sea fishing industry has confronted over the past 50 years. They were forced to stay one step ahead of changes in the international situation and look for new fishing grounds, without any time to let their guard down.

Impact of the Second Oil Shocks

After stabilizing in the wake of the first oil shocks, oil prices were shaken up again in 1978 when Iran announced that it would cease all exports of crude oil. This led to another shock that caused the price to jump from $12.70 per barrel to $34. Combined with the economic downturn that struck Korea in 1979, the Bu-Ma Democratic Protests against the Yushin regime and the assassination of President Park Chung-hee caused the country to enter a state of serious stagflation. In 1980, Korea's economic growth rate was −5.1%, the first negative figure on record since the country had started to develop.

Some reports from that time outline the difficulties faced by the deep sea fishing industry. An article published in the Dong-a Ilbo on June 24, 1980 described the scores of ships that had given up on fishing and returned to Busan Port to be sold.

During this period, it was Kim Jae-chul's robust hauls that allowed Dongwon to maintain steady growth. When Kim saw the first signs of recession, he had decided to move into more labor-saving, technology-intensive sectors of the industry, which ended up paying dividends.

Kwon Yeong-ho, the CEO of Inter-Burgo Group who hailed from an engineering background and had built a large corporate empire, once said "I do not envy people like Carnegie or Warren Buffet. The only man I envy and respect is Dongwon Group's president, Kim Jae-chul."

Part III

Business Expansion and Crises

story 1

Expanding the Business and Seizing Opportunities

The Path to Business Expansion

"Those that abandon their main business end up in ruin, and the same is true of those who fail to explore other avenues. In any moment, the wind speed can pick up to a level far above the average wind speed. If you need a ship that can hold one ton, then build one that can withstand five tons. Companies also need to look out for crises in advance. When the crisis is upon you, it's already too late." This is a quote from Kim Jae-chul.

Doing Business Means Never Taking Your Feet off the Pedals

Even when his tuna longlining business was flourishing, Kim continued to seek out new avenues of growth. He looked beyond the maritime industry, founding a general foods company and seizing opportunities in the finance industry to great success.

A Weak Start Leads to a New Path

Using the capital he had accumulated, Kim sought out new projects that would complement his fishing business. He eventually chose cold storage of maritime products, an area he was already well-versed in. He bought a 16,500 square meter plot of land in Busan, and founded Dongwon Cold Storage in 1976. Throughout this process, Kim paid attention to four points.

① Fish caught at sea required cold storage facilities in order to be sold at full price

② In many cases, a lack of cold storage facilities meant that fish was unable to be unloaded in good time, and this problem needed to be solved.

③ By becoming involved in the distribution industry through cold storage facilities, it would be possible to create a new source of revenue.

④ From 1985, Dongwon Cold Storage began producing its own frozen mackerel for use as tuna bait, and also supplied the product to other companies. This confirmed the potential that existed in the distribution, marine products processing an manufacturing industries.

Issuing a Challenge to General Food Companies

Kim opened a Dongwon Industries foodstuffs store in Seongnam, Gyeonggi Province, boosting the freshness of fish caught in the northern seas and directly selling to consumers in the capital area. The establishment of the Foods Division was an important decision that helped to create the Dongwon Group of today.

As the foodstuffs store grew, it was eventually split off into an independent company, Dongwon Foods. The business included cold storage and deep freezing, as well as the retailing and wholesaling of agricultural and maritime products.

By firmly establishing itself in the market for processed foods such as seasoned laver, crab meat and fish cakes, Dongwon Foods helped Dongwon Group to grow into a general foods company. The company later merged with the newly launched Dongwon F&B in 2000.

Kim ran Dongwon Industries and Dongwon Foods separately because he viewed them as completely different businesses. He once said the following.

"The fishing industry and manufacturing industry deal with completely different things. As long as your hands stay wet with seawater, the fishing industry will continue to be profitable. Regardless of how much a ship costs, you can make up for it with unlimited credit. This is why people lack a sound understanding of management principles and the concept of cost of production. On the other hand, the manufacturing industry needs to work hard every step of the way and make meticulous plans. So those who have worked in the fishing industry don't perform very well in the processing industry. Fishermen try to solve everything in a single sweep."

From Catching Fish to Marine Product Processing and Distribution

Kim also seized a new opportunity in canned tuna. The canned tuna market was born out of the concepts of 'gap' (a person in a position of power) and 'eul' (a person in a subordinate position). In any transaction, parties were completely reliant on their partner and had to lay all of their cards on the table. In the early days of the purse seining business, Kim exported the entirety of his catch to StarKist, a US canned tuna firm. This naturally led to problems since StarKist had a monopoly on demand. In short, Kim had to supply fish at the price set by StarKist.

In any line of business, it is risky to rely too heavily on a single entity as a source of revenue. Kim knew that if he failed to find additional clients, he would have difficulty selling his catch even if he managed to haul in more fish.

Producing Canned Tuna, A New Product Line

After completing an AMP course at Harvard in 1981, Kim stopped off at the StarKist factory in Los Angeles on his way back to Korea. "We could run a factory like this," he thought to himself.

"I didn't know whether there would be enough demand for such a product in Korea, but after conducting some research, I learned that demand for canned tuna usually began when per capita income reached $2,000 in a country. At the time, Korea's per capita income was around $1,300, so I thought it was worth giving the business a try. I made a loss at the beginning, but the market started to expand rapidly around the time of the Seoul Olympics." Kim was an innovator that brought canned tuna to Korea as a new product line.

Claiming Victory amidst Fierce Competition

Around that time, a newspaper article described the fierce competition taking place in the canned tuna market in the following terms.

However, Dongwon Industries retained an average market share of 72.6% up until 2013, selling more than 200 million cans per year. In July 2014, local media reported "Dongwon Tuna, the people's choice among tuna brands, is the first fishery product brand to reach five billion cans in sales, setting a new record."

Venturing into Finance

The success of Korea Investment Holdings, which continued to grow rapidly after being divested from Dongwon Group in 2003, was a landmark achievement in Kim's business career.

After making a clear distinction between the things he was good at and the things he was not, Kim pushed ahead with the split and boldly placed the firm under independent management. Kim's management philosophy of "Entrusting things I don't know to people who know better" proved to be a success in this case.

A Gift from Studying at Harvard

At the time Kim left to study at Harvard, the purse seining business, which entailed massive risks, had not yet become firmly established.

"I took an AMP course at Seoul National University, and I kept hearing about the 'Harvard case study.' Nowadays we live in an era of information, so it would be easy to figure out what that means without actually traveling there, but that wasn't the case back in those days. So I resolved to find the time to travel to the US and hear about the Harvard case study for myself. One of the key takeaways from the Harvard course was the potential that existed in the securities industry. I had no idea, and was surprised to see that most of America's brightest students were jumping into finance."

Kim learned two things from his course at Harvard. The first was that the securities industry was worth getting involved in, and the second was the commercial potential of canned tuna.

Venturing into the Securities Industry with Five Billion in Reserves

Kim Jae-chul's entry into the securities business came about when he seized an opportunity caused by changing times in Korea. In line with the privatization guidelines for commercial banks that came into effect in 1981, Hanshin Securities was up for sale. Alongside Sambo Securities and Dongyang Securities, Hanshin was one of Korea's leading securities firm at the time. It was believed that a bid in the range of seven billion KRW would be successful, but Dongwon Industries only had two billion KRW in capital at the time.

However, Dongwon also had a substantial amount of

internal reserves, and believed that the investment was worth it. This was possible also because if the firm's assets were reappraised, it would be a sound company worth several times the value of its capital. However, with so many differences between investing in a securities firm and purchasing a ship, Kim only understood half of the story.

Acquiring Hanshin Securities and Scouting Kim Jung-tae, a Financial Wonder Kid

Kim Jae-chul worked hard for ten years to turn the securities firm into a success, and it was Kim Jung-tae (former CEO of Kookmin Bank) and Park Hyeon-ju (CEO of Mirae Asset Securities) that played a pivotal role in this process. In particular, Kim recruited the young finance whiz Kim Jung-tae in 1986 when he was only 36, and the pair of them worked together for 17 years.

Kim Jung-tae sent a wave of fresh air through the Korean financial world with incentives, transparent management, zero debt management and stock options systems, and all of these experiments took place at Dongwon Securities. After serving as the CEO of Dongwon Securities, he was recruited to serve as the CEO of Korea Housing Bank in 1997 at the age of 51, where he once again lived up to his name. Sad to see him go, Kim Jae-chul offered him a hefty farewell gift and said the following. "Do what you believe in. If it doesn't work then you can always come back." The two have remained on good terms since then.

While Kim was fortunate enough to form good relationships with people like Kim Jung-tae, there were other occasions where people took staff members with them and dealt a severe blow to the company. Although it was a painful experience in the moment, everything was forgotten as time passed.

"Meeting people and bidding farewell are part of life. When someone departs, you should endeavor to leave them with a good impression. Whether good or bad, saying goodbye is not the end. There is often a lasting impact and traces that linger for a long time.

Kim paid particular attention to this point whenever he switched jobs during his youth. One example that comes to mind is Kim's connection with Lee Hak-su, the CEO of Korea Wonyang Fisheries. Six months before leaving the company, Kim made his intentions clear and took care to ensure the firm did not suffer any damage, which allowed him to remain on good terms with Lee until he passed away. To Kim Jae-chul, credit refers to not only financial promises, but also the trust that comes from not letting other people.

Doing Business in an Unfamiliar Field

In the early stages, Dongwon Industries continued to invest in securities, but it was difficult to grow the business. Hanshin Securities had five billion KRW in capital when it was acquired by Dongwon in 1982, but this figure had grown to 45 billion KRW by 1988 and 179.5 billion KRW by 1995.

On the other hand, Dongwon Securities remained 4th or 5th in the industry rankings up until the 1990s, but developed into a leading firm when vice president Kim Nam-goo took the reins as CEO.

Kim Jae-chul learned several things while running the securities firm, and also went through some changes.

One of these was his attitude towards investing in staff. Kim's view on personnel had been simple when he worked in the fishing industry in the 1970s. "I need to look out for the people who joined the company because they trusted me, so I should only take on and train as many staff as I need."

However, after acquiring the securities firm, Kim realized that a single person could perform the work of 1,000 or even 10,000, which made him more determined to invest in his staff.

The fundamental differences between fishing and securities called for a different approach to management.

While Kim's insistence on keeping the two fields separate was a factor that contributed to his success, he always thought that "the securities business is for young people."

The Launch of Korea Investment Holdings

Kim changed the name of Hanshin Securities to Dongwon Securities. By focusing on internal stability from 1996 onwards, including zero debt management, Kim was better equipped than other securities firms to handle the Asian Financial Crisis of the late 1990s. While other companies suffered from major losses, Dongwon Securities posted a profit of 18.6 billion KRW.

After Kim's eldest son, Kim Nam-goo, completed his MBA at Keio University in Japan, he joined Hansin Securities as an assistant manager and received training in corporate management. Kim had planned to divest the finance business from the outset, and he gifted 550,000 of his Dongwon Industries shares to Kim Nam-goo.

This was a major news item at the time, because he had to pay 6.2 billion KRW in gift taxes on the transfer of shares to his son. The National Tax Service claimed it was the largest amount of self-reported gift tax on record, excluding taxes that had been levied after an investigation by authorities. This event, which embodied Kim's life philosophy of not being stingy, was featured in the headlines of Korean newspapers once the National Tax Service informed the media.

In particular, an editorial in the *Chosun Ilbo* noted, "we should never forget that Kim's voluntary payment of gift tax is the largest amount ever recorded. Although well-known families of Korea's *chaebol*, or large conglomerates, have paid their share of inheritance and gift taxes in a legitimate way, the large amount paid by Kim is unprecedented. To think of the fact that there are so many people who own businesses much bigger than Kim's and are much wealthier than him in Korea, it is highly likely that they evaded taxes by paying much less. It is said that paying a mere 10% as inheritance and gift tax is more than expected. No matter what the truth is, it's inspiring that Dongwon followed Kim' s belief and morality of staying true to principles even when there are numerous way of dodging taxes."

By establishing an investment holdings company and separating it from Dongwon Group in 2003, Dongwon is now fully independent in terms of both stocks and management decision-making.

Korea Investment Holdings has now developed into a major financial group. As of 2014, the company was the parent of six subsidiaries including Korea Investment & Securities, Korea Investment Management Co, Korea Investment Value Asset Management Co, Korea Investment Savings Bank and Korea Investment Partners. These subsidiaries in turn had 16 subsidiaries and five overseas offices of their own. Korea Investment & Securities was the top ranked securities in firm in terms of net profits for four consecutive years from 2011.

Working to Expand the Business Horizons

"After the captain, the next most important thing to think about is the fishing grounds." Kim's view on the meaning of corporate expansion can be summed up as "Where is the next fishing ground (market) located?" CEO compares the role of a CEO to that of a ship's captain.

Entrepreneurs always talk in terms of results. "It is not advisable for entrepreneurs to appear in the news too often, because that means you are not working hard enough." This comment speaks to the importance of focusing all of one' s energy on getting results. In other words, an entrepreneur is someone who is able to speak about their achievements in figures.

Advancing into the Manufacturing Industry

Kim Jae-chul's second business venture was into manufacturing, a sector with no relation to the maritime industry. Kim invested a lot of money in Orion Optics, which he founded in 1977, but the project ended in failure.

It is interesting to note that he also failed to achieve much success in service industries such as the restaurant business. Kim believes that these poor results are due to the fact that he couldn't hire the right people.

"When I tried doing business in the services industry, the first few stores performed well. But you need a bigger team to expand beyond that point, and it was hard to find the right people. You need to have the right people before starting the business. Whenever I tried to launch the business first and then hire people, the project usually failed to achieve much success."

From Marine Product Processing to a General Food Company

When the Guryongpo factory began producing frozen fillets in 1986, it was the company's first self-owned factory. With the acquisition of the Guryongpo facility and the construction of a new processing plant in Gwangju, Kim expanded his business portfolio to include seasoned squid, seasoned fish cakes, crab meat and raw fish bait for tuna. This helped to establish Dongwon as a marine product processing firm.

The company continued to expand and develop into a general food company, becoming involved in the processing of agricultural and marine products. Economic growth and changing dietary patterns towards greater convenience in Korea led to rapid growth in the frozen foods market, and Kim picked up on this trend, founding Dongil Frozen Foods in 1978. The company began to mass produce dumplings, croquettes, pork cutlets and fried foods.

One of his main partners was Nissui, a Japanese frozen foods and general marine products firm. Deep sea fishing accounted for less than 30% of Nissui's revenue. The company had invested in food-related fields such as pharmaceuticals and health foods, building a successful business portfolio.

In 1991, Dongwon founded Samyang Industrial Co, which produced canned tuna, as well as Cheongju Foods, a dedicated manufacturer of seasoned laver. The company also acquired Hansung Feeds, a producer of assorted feeds. This was followed by the acquisition of organic businesses E-Farm and Dongwon Wine Plus in 2003, DM Food in 2005, the manufacturing, processing and sales division of Haitai

Dairy in 2006 and dedicated seasoned foods manufacturer Samjo Celtech in 2007.

A New Axis of Growth in Packaging Materials

"Aren't there any new lines of business?" This was a question that Kim Jae-chul has continued to pose to both himself and others throughout his life as he searched for an answer. Even now, past the age of 80, Kim continues to ask this question and seek out new challenges. He has recently been taking active steps in the food packaging materials industry.

He approached the packaging materials business from the perspective of strengthening the competitiveness of Dongwon's main businesses and generating a new source of revenue. Samyang Industrial Co was established in 1991 as a producer of tupperware for cans, and Dongwon also founded Dongwon Precision in 1990 as a dedicated manufacturer of plastic containers.

Packaging materials became an established source of growth for Kim in 1999, when he acquired a Naon factory that was up for sale in Jincheon, North Chungcheon

Province. This factory produced paper cups, and was on the market for 2.4 billion KRW, yet people seemed to be taking little interest. After making a number of bids, Kim acquired the factory for one billion KRW, and this facility came to serve as the foundation for Dongwon Group's packaging business, which later achieved sales of more than one trillion KRW.

"The packaging materials industry is larger in scale and more diverse than the fishing business, and I thought that there would be greater demand as the family structures have become much more fragmented. In 2013, Dongwon acquired Daehan Eunpakgy, a producer of aluminum foil. The following year, the company also bought Hanjin P&C, a company that owned patents for the production of industrial film, industrial printers and cardboard boxes.

Originally founded in 1971, Hanjin P&C possessed a high level of technology and supplied glass-protecting film to Corning in the US, Taiwan and Korea. Through M&As, Dongwon Systems obtained manufacturing technology and professional staff from across all sectors of the packaging materials business including soft materials, other materials

(PET bottles, plastic containers and other plasticware), aluminum processing and resins.

Although subsidiaries accounted for around 60% of packaging materials revenue up until 2010, by 2014 this proportion had dropped to below 20%. This demonstrates that packaging materials had become established as a key axis of growth within Dongwon Group.

"Dongwon Group has three main growth engines - deep sea fishing, food processing and packaging materials. Dongwon Systems is currently the leading Korean packaging materials company in terms of market share."

Acquiring StarKist, Kim's Former Ruler

Kim Jae-chul was the first captain to supply fish to StarKist in Samoa. Thanks to this connection, he was invited to a commemorative ceremony on the company's 20th anniversary in 1983. However, by the time the company's 50th anniversary celebration came around, Kim attended the event as a majority shareholder in the company.

Although StarKist was the leading firm in the US canned tuna market, the company meant more to Kim than simply market value or market share. StarKist had ruled over Kim for some time. While there were many people in the fishing business, the only buyers of tuna in Samoa at that time were StarKist and Van camp's.

Developing into a Global Company

With the acquisition of StarKist, Dongwon Group was able to expand its purchasing and manufacturing strengths from the Korean market to the global market. The Dongwon F&B factory in Changwon is currently the world's largest producer of canned tuna.

Dongwon applied the same innovations to the StarKist factory, reducing the number of staff required at the plant from 2,900 to 1,900 through an additional investment of $30 million. This innovation helped to make StarKist profitable once again.

As StarKist's reputation improved after the acquisition, the company was able to recruit talented staff and instill the company's vision in all employees, giving them the motivation to develop into global talent. As StarKist's financial situation stabilized, the company's market value soared to twice the price that Dongwon had paid for it. The successful acquisition of a foreign firm by a Korean company also served to accelerate Korea's entry into overseas markets.

Kim's experience of acquiring StarKist and applying innovation to the company led him to put forward a new proposal for university education in Korea. When he saw engineers from the Changwon factory being sent to work in the StarKist factory, Kim identified the potential for engineers educated in Korea to play a greater role in the global market.

"We needed to send students from polytechnic universities to work as technicians in overseas manufacturers. It was difficult to find employment overseas, but we managed to send thousands of Korean engineers abroad. That was the path for helping young Koreans go abroad," he stressed.

A Holding Company for Responsible and Transparent Management

"We were practically the first holding company in Korea."

Right from the outset, Kim believed that business of a different nature should be run separately in order to ensure that they were managed responsibly and transparently.

However, most companies were unable to set up a holding company even if they had the will to do so, due to tight-knit relations between stockholders and the comparatively low ratio of stocks held by controlling shareholders.

The main advantage of a holding company structure is that the holding company can focus on investments while the original companies remain dedicated to their respective businesses, which promotes simplicity and greater transparency in corporate governance. Holdings companies are also able to accurately assess the performance of subsidiaries, contributing to the maximization of corporate value. Other benefits include enabling shareholder-focused management and facilitating corporate restructuring through the early disposal of insolvent subsidiaries, attracting foreign capital and entering new lines of business.

Dongwon Group is a general goods industry group that consists of 18 main subsidiaries, centered around Dongwon Enterprises. Korea Investment Holdings exists separately from Dongwon Enterprises. This company is the parent of 15 subsidiaries including Korea Investment & Securities, Dongwon Securities and Korea Investment Management

Co. Not a single share between the two holding companies is cross-owned, and they are completely independent in legal and management terms.

Dongwon Group's Process of Diversification

As the world's top deep sea fishing company, Dongwon Industries had no choice but to continually reinvent itself to survive in a rapidly changing environment. To achieve this, the company had to diversify its portfolio.

During this process, Kim Jae-chul refused to adopt the reckless credit-based expansion strategy that was customary in the financial world at the time. In other words, Kim chose a new growth model in which each subsidiary in the Dongwon Group family was managed independently, without any cross-ownership or share swaps.

story 2

A Business Crisis and Learning from Failure

Shaken by the Asian Financial Crisis

The 1997 Asian Financial Crisis was an unprecedented shock of epic proportions. Seventeen of the 30 major corporate groups in Korea dissolved, and Kim was caught in the crossfire as well. However, he was able to sniff out the signs of the looming financial crisis in advance.

"As I wish you a happy new year, I can't help but think that we will face great difficulties this year. However, looking back over the past decades, we have encountered and overcome many hardships. Although I believe that the difficulties that confront us will not be easy to solve, as they are the result of longstanding internal problems that will spill over to the surface, I am certain that the Korean people will be able to adeptly overcome these challenges if we are cognizant of them, precisely because the underlying causes can be found at home. History shows us that conquering great difficulties leads to great development."

The foresight shown by one businessman ten months prior to the beginning of the financial crisis is truly astonishing. The basis on which Kim reached this conclusion was the alarm bells that were ringing for Dongwon Industries, which had experienced rapid growth since its inception and was Korea's top exporter in the deep sea fishing industry. Dongwon Industries recorded its first ever loss in 1996.

"On this occasion, we are preparing ourselves for a new beginning in 1997. However, the journey ahead of us will not be smooth. With the company posting a loss last year for the first time in its 28-year history, I must apologize to all our hardworking staff because we were unable to hand out the end of year bonuses that were promised. If we worked so hard, why did we end up in the red? It is because we became complacent in our old ways of working, while the environment around us greatly changed."

The Insolvency of Dongwon Finance Burdens the Whole Group

Although the general consensus was that the loss posted by Dongwon Industries was a temporary phenomenon caused by poor fishing conditions and the acquisition of new vessels, Kim felt a unique sense of crisis.

He stopped lecturing outside the company, quit playing golf and took time for self-reflection, with the mindset that he would have to turn over a new leaf. Even though he had achieved dozens of successes, he was well aware that everything could collapse in the face of a single crisis.

In addition to the financial deficit, another crisis was looming for Dongwon Industries. As Korea's credit rating plummeted due to the financial crisis, rolling over debt became an impossibility. This was a substantial burden, compounded by the rapid deterioration of the Korean Won.

In 1997 alone, losses on foreign currency valuations amounted to 64.5 billion KRW, since most of the funds that Kim had borrowed to build his ships were denominated in foreign currency.

Even worse, Dongwon's financial business was suddenly struck by great misfortune. After acquiring Hanshin Factoring in 1995 for 10 billion KRW, Kim had changed the company name to Dongwon Finance, and the firm had grown into a large factoring company with capital of close to 65 billion KRW after three rounds of recapitalization. The company was the industry leader in terms of capital and sales performance, recording an operating profit of 83.5 billion KRW in 1997.

At the time, Dongwon Finance had taken out substantial bank loans to build golf courses, but there was a string of bankruptcies among golf courses when the financial crisis struck. Dongwon Industries was in such a poor state that rumors circulated about the company joining the list of bankruptcies. At that point, there was a savior who lent a helping hand to Kim Jae-chul.

In 1998, Dongwon brought in a record-breaking haul of tuna, the price jumped from $800 per ton to $1,200, and Kim also benefited from the skyrocketing exchange rate. In April 1998, the company hauled in 12,000 tons, the highest figure on record since its inception.

"I received help from God. I built my life on the sea, and it was the sea that saved me in my time of need." In June 1998, Dongwon Industries' 24.2 billion KRW loss from the previous year had transformed into a 31.8 billion KRW profit. Over the same period, the company's debt to equity ratio fell from 484% to 198%.

The credit Dongwon had built up over the years also played an important role. At a point when not a penny of foreign currency could be spared, Mitsubishi stepped in to help out.

The Power of Swift Crisis Management

Another factor that helped Kim weather the storm was the success of his company's financial section. When Director Kim Nam-goo received a call from a friend in Hong Kong who told him that the financial crisis in Southeast Asia would soon spread to Japan, he immediately moved to take action. He sold off most of the company's marketable securities to obtain 300 billion KRW in funds. Thanks to this swift response, Dongwon Securities was able to boost its profits even in the midst of the crisis, which served as a buffer for the group.

Learning from Failure

"When a captain boards only good ships, it is difficult to learn all the ins and outs. But if you take a broken vessel and repair it in the docks of a shipyard, you learn every aspect of the ship's structure."

When Kim Jae-chul determined that one of his new endeavors was a failure, he made bold decisions instead of dwelling on the past. He never fell victim to the 'sunk cost fallacy,' where a person sinks deeper into a hole because of prior investment.

A Cycle of Challenge and Failure

Memories of both success and failure are valuable. Although Kim showed great enthusiasm for the camera business when he established Orion Optics in 1977, he lost a lot of money on the project. Other failed endeavors include his wireless communications business through Happy Telecom and a foray into the electronics industry through the acquisition of Sungmi Electronics. Kim also entered the restaurant business, but was unable to achieve the results he was looking for.

The First Unrelated Business: Orion Optics

Ever since the early days, Kim had taken an interest in the manufacturing sector, because success on the ocean was dependent on the natural environment. He made up his mind to take on the precision optics industry, believing that exporting a small volume would be easy if he was successfully able to localize technology acquired from Japan.

Kim was certain of the commercial viability of cameras, and when he saw Japan catch up to Germany, the original creator of the technology, and become a leading producer of cameras, he believed that Korea could do the same.

In addition to this, he did not think there was a high probability of large corporations entering the industry, since famous Japanese camera makers such as Asahi Pentax, Canon and Minolta were all small to medium-sized enterprises. Finally, Kim believed that Koreans were skilled with their hands and well-suited to the precision industry.

The company began producing interchangeable lenses,

multi-coated lenses and 600X biological microscopes in 1978, with Pentax cameras added to the production line in 1984. After completing KS registration for 'Orion Microscopes,' sales of Dongwon's products climbed to the extent that the company obtained 30% of the domestic market.

However, after launching the business, Kim realized that cameras contained more components than he had originally thought, and there were no Korean manufacturers of such components.

"Korea did not have a single company equipped with shutter, lens or coating technology. The final blow came when large corporations entered the industry. When Samsung began to sell cameras, their credit sales went through the roof. It turns out it takes more than just an idea and passion to start a business."

A Small Foray into Manufacturing through Textiles

The textiles industry was another attempt by Kim Jae-chul to lay a manufacturing foundation for Dongwon.

He launched the business by building a new textiles factory

in Seongnam Industrial Complex and signing a technical cooperation and sales contract with Shikishima Textiles, but canned the project when it proved to be unprofitable.

You cannot rush into an industry just because it looks promising, and success is improbable without a team of people who are well-versed in the field and willing to work hard as if the company was their own. When the textiles business failed to work out, Kim reformed his textiles division into a fur division, but the poor performances of this business caused him to wring his hands of textiles altogether.

Venturing into Telecommunications Equipment: Sungmi Electronics

With the advent of the internet, the 1990s promised a new age of ICT development. Kim acquired Sungmi Electronics in 1995. As a listed telecommunications equipment company, Sungmi was a financially sound firm with 116.9 billion KRW in sales and a net profit of eight billion KRW. The company continued to grow smoothly in the first few years after the acquisition.

However, this growth proved to be short-lived. Kim had

overestimated the company's core capacities. Most of the company's profit model was based on selling products imported from overseas. In other words, the company's main competency was in sales rather than technology. With foreign-made telecommunications equipment flowing into Korea through a number of channels, the company began to struggle with declining sales. The fact that the management team had been replaced with people who were not fit for the job after the acquisition also contributed to the company's woes.

Sungmi's sales, which amounted to 350 billion KRW in 2000, dropped to 200 billion KRW in 2001, with the 16.7 billion KRW net profit plummeting to a 68.2 billion KRW deficit.

The main reasons for Kim's failure in this case were investing in a field he knew nothing about and failing to secure the right people. The price he paid for this failure is a valuable lesson that should be heeded by anyone attempting a merger or acquisition today.

A Foray into Telecommunications Services: Happy Telecom

"In the beginning, I planned to focus on growing a single business instead of trying my hand in several different fields. But corporate management is all about adjusting to the environment, and I changed my mind, believing that I had to keep up with the changing times. So I wanted to run specialized, mobile businesses in a number of fields. From that perspective, I planned to found a lot of specialized companies."

In line with this view, Kim thought that the mobile telecommunications services sector looked promising, and tossed his hat into the ring with a Seoul-based pager company in 1992. Dongwon Industries Consortium looked like a promising candidate during the screening process, but the company was ultimately eliminated in the final screening.

"For some reason, the company's score fell from second place to third place at the last minute. To get past that would have required asking for a few favors, and that was something I was not very good at."

The Importance of Timing

At the time, Kim believed that entering the telecommunications services industry was akin to a golden goose that would redefine the landscape of the business world. Although his conclusion was correct, things did not work out as he had expected.

Nevertheless, during the second round of selections for pager service providers in the capital area in 1996, Kim successfully obtained a business license. However, it turned out that rushing into business in Seoul was not a wise choice, because the center of the wireless telecommunications market began to shift toward mobile phones at a faster pace than expected. Although it was not an easy decision, Kim had no choice but to dust off his hands and walk away from the business in which he had invested and increased the capital to 20 billion KRW.

Learning from Strategic Withdrawal

"A business venture may not work out as well as you thought it would. When that happens, it's important to get out of the business." This can be difficult to do when there is a large sunk cost, and the more you have invested, the harder it is to walk away. Kim is very firm on this point. He has strategically pulled out of many projects over the years, including flatfish aquaculture and squid processing on Jeju Island, producing animated films, an MIT project, the restaurant business and the courier business.

Flatfish Aquaculture

The flatfish aquaculture business was first launched by Kim Jae-chul on Jeju Island. Although Kim backed out after the venture proved to be unsuccessful, he left behind a solid flatfish aquaculture business in Jeju.

Prior to Kim's idea of conducting large-scale aquaculture on land, the business of raising fish referred to cultivating fish in an enclosed section of the sea. A request from Jeju Island was one of the main drivers behind his decision to set up an aquaculture farm on the island.

Over three rounds of investment, Kim injected 8 billion KRW to construct an aquaculture building and nursery facilities on a beach in Namjeju-gun, Jeju. The facilities were equipped to raise 200 tons of fish per year. This was the first corporate aquaculture business that cultivated flatfish, pufferfish, rockfish and sea bass. However, after several years of operation the facility had failed to prove its commercial viability. When Kim looked into the reason behind this, he was surprised to learn that the problem lay in the fish food.

Flatfish are nervous creatures that are very sensitive to temperature and oxygen levels. They often suffered from digestive diseases when fed refrigerated food. In addition to this, the workers often moved the flatfish around to classify them into groups based on size without any consideration for their nature. This process caused great stress to the captive fish. Kim also discovered that water was not flowing properly through some of the drainage pipes.

When Kim visited the facility to identify the reasons behind these problems, he also unearthed a number of management issues. First of all, there was no cooperation at all between the Aquaculture Department, Business Department and Management Department.

Second, most of the experts with university degrees insisted on performing office work, leaving only the laborers to work in the actual farms. Kim determined that these problems were not unique to the Jeju facility, and decided to perform an investigation on the whole company.

At this time, up to 100 aquaculture farms popped up nearby, but just when the business was starting to become established, people started criticizing large corporations for throwing their weight around in the industry. When Kim heard this, he decided to wring his hands of the business altogether.

The name 'Jeju Flounder' has now become known as a brand name. This was the business that Kim Jae-chul left behind in Jeju. As of 2013, there were 351 aquaculture farms in Jeju Island, with annual production of 260 billion KRW, accounting for 62% of Korea's flatfish production.

The Restaurant Business: Dongga

When Dongwon began selling tuna for domestic use in 1991, Kim had a positive view of raw tuna. Raw tuna restaurants began to spring up like mushrooms in cities across Korea, and Dongwon Industries was one of the first movers in the restaurant industry. However, Kim failed to achieve much success in the franchise business. Later on,

Dongwon F&B acquired Sandpresso and continues to run the business today.

Other Withdrawals

When conducting business, it is inevitable that you will face unforeseen circumstances. When Dongsu Co, the firm that had shared an office with Kim when he first founded Dongwon Industries, began to experience financial difficulties, he put another of his business ideas into action by purchasing the Guryongpo factory and starting frozen fillet production in 1985. The product was processed squid with seasoning.

The Odaegam Seasoned Fish Episode

The brand name 'Odaegam Seasoned Fish' was chosen for the seasoned squid, and the launch of the product was accompanied by an aggressive marketing campaign. Even now, the advertisement is a delight to watch. The scene, which featured a ridiculous-looking man named Oh Daegam in a sedan chair holding a sign that read 'Odaegam Seasoned Fish,' was very popular at the time.

The Guryongpo factory was equipped with facilities capable of producing four million pieces per year. However, an unexpected problem occurred. An official clan of people surnamed 'Oh' came out in protest against the ad, claiming that it was disrespectful to associate their ancestors with squid. This was not limited to a single region, and the protests could soon spread to Oh clans across the country. In the face of such a backlash, Kim decided to scrap the project. This experience taught Kim that no matter how thorough your preparation, there will always be unforeseen problems.

The MIT Business, Opposed by Everyone

Kim Jae-chul has shown a propensity for making bold investments in promising new technology. One example is when the Electronics and Telecommunications Research Institute's MIT research team developed the world's first new material that could turn insulators into metals that conduct electricity, breaking the conventional wisdom that electricity could not flow through insulators (semiconductors). Dongwon signed a technology transfer agreement for the technology with a deposit of 2 billion KRW, and began to work on the new business. Kim predicted that this product would lead to the creation of a market worth more than 1 trillion KRW per year, but the process of commercializing the technology was ultimately unsuccessful.

I asked him why he chose to invest at a time when many related institutions and companies were shying away from the technology. "You have to pay your dues to find new growth engines," he replied. "Even now, I continue to pay my dues." A pioneering spirit, willingness to experiment and the vigor of youth are still driving forces in Kim's life. He is still a dreamer that is awed by new technologies and state-of-the-art industries.

Lessons from Crises and Failures

Kim summarizes what he learned from failure under the following ten points.

① A business can fail at any time. Don't become arrogant when things are going well, you should never lose focus on your business.

② Do not be overwhelmed by crises, you must get through them by thinking about what comes afterwards. Once you weather the storm, a large fishing ground will appear before your eyes.

③ Credit is your relief pitcher during a crisis. In a capitalist society, credit is money.

④ An inaccurate understanding of the essence of your business will end in failure.

⑤ How much do you stand to lose in the worst-case scenario? What impact would it have on other affiliated companies? You should check the answers to these questions using figures, and then check again to make sure.

⑥ Be careful to avoid getting blinded by greed. You should only start new businesses to the extent that you can manage the risk.

⑦ The success or failure of a new business hinges on having the right people.

⑧ Managers must know how to listen to the minority opinion. This is especially true for making decisions about new businesses. Kim is wary about the dogmatic decision-making of many successful people. Those who have achieved great success can also end up failing spectacularly.

⑨ Stubbornly sticking to an incorrect decision is a shortcut to failure. You need the wisdom to get out while you can rather than becoming attached to your decision.

⑩ You need to put limits in place when taking on new challenges. This includes a promise to pull out of the venture once you reach a certain level of losses.

Part IV

Kim Jae-chul's Management Philosophy and Methods

story 1

Management Principles and Attitude

A Philosophical Leader

Both people and businesses need a philosophy. Although it is possible to earn money in the short-term through trickery or good fortune, companies that seek to go the distance must have a clear philosophy.

Living with Faith and Sincerity

As the eldest son of a large family who grew up in a poor rural area, Kim held a firm belief that he needed to take responsibility for himself and his family. This sphere of responsibility later expanded to include his company, society and his country.

Kim believes that anything can be sacrificed in order to meet one's responsibilities. Ever since his youth, Kim has lived in a fierce world of professionals.

Achieving Social Justice through Earnest Corporate Activities (Kim's corporate mission when he founded Dongwon)

To Kim, a company is an entity that earns profits, generates jobs and pays taxes. He often says "Corporate management is about contributing to humanity and the state, so making a loss is a sin. My corporate philosophy is 'righteous management.'"

On the 24th anniversary of the company's establishment in July 1993, a 'Progress Rally for the Announcement of Dongwon's Value System and Management Innovation' was held in which Dongwon's corporate vision was declared to be 'a socially necessary enterprise that generates new value.'

A Propelling Spirit of Corporate Management

Kim's life and corporate management are supported by four key values. Enthusiasm, a frontier spirit, personal development and righteous management.

The Importance of Enthusiasm

Enthusiasm refers to the attitude of putting your heart and soul into achieving the best result for the task you have been assigned. Kim never put in a half-hearted effort, whether it was his own business or another role he had been assigned, such as at a trade association.

A competent person is someone who achieves good results.

Results = ability x effort x thoughts. In other words, no matter how much talent you may have, it means nothing without hard work. Ability and effort must also be employed in the right direction. It is also worth noting that this equation features multiplication rather than addition. If even one of the variables is a negative, the answer will also come out negative.

The Importance of a Frontier Spirit

According to Kim, a 'frontier spirit' refers to the mindset of seeking to open new horizons, even if that means creating a path that didn't exist before. He stresses the following points.

"I have reached this point in life through the mindset of forging my own path if one doesn't exist. In 1975, I built the Dongsan by investing more money than my company was worth at the time. During the second round of oil shocks, I once again took the risk of loading a helicopter on the Costa de Marfil tuna purse seiner.

The ships I invested in during that period played a large part in helping Dongwon Industries grow into the world' s top fisheries company. I was able to make those decisions because I had the confidence that even if I failed, I could always get back on board a ship as a captain and earn at least enough to take care of my family. When I asked Kim what the Dongwon spirit is, he did not hesitate to answer "Enthusiasm and challenge."

The Importance of Personal Development

Kim's academic history shows that he completed Korea University's CEO course in 1969, Seoul National University's CEO course in 1978 and Harvard's CEO course at a later date, all so that he could stay on top of new trends and learn the latest management techniques. Kim's zeal for learning has not abated even though he is now past the age of 80.

The Importance of Righteous Management

Righteous management refers to not only operating within the boundaries of the law, but also acting in a way that absolves you from criticism for being unethical. Kim draws a clear distinction between fields he is capable in and those he should not touch.

One example is when Kim suddenly became the center of attention due to one politician's slip of the tongue. Politician K from the Democratic Party once claimed that Kim had provided 5 billion KRW to Roh Moo-hyun when he was running for president.

In spite of efforts to dissuade him from doing so, Kim appeared before a hearing in the National Assembly and fought against every aspect of the allegations, even filing a lawsuit against an incumbent member of the National Assembly. When the Ministry of Justice finally cleared his name, Kim withdrew the legal claims once he received an official apology from his accusers. This incident speaks to Kim Jae-chul's lifelong commitment to righteous management, and should serve as a lesson for the business leaders of today.

story 2

Management Methods and Tools

How to Get Results through Action

Stick to Your Principles

The two principles on which Kim Jae-chul will not budge are acting with integrity and keeping promises.

The following story took place in the early days of his business At the time, Kim had loaned a fishing vessel from a Japanese general trading firm on the condition that he would pay the money back three installments over the course of a year.

Interest rates were high during that period, and Kim could earn a significant amount of money by delaying the payments by a month or two. However, irrespective of common practice at the time, Kim made sure that he never missed a payment. He believed that acting with integrity would build up a bank of credit that would serve as an asset for earning even more money in the future.

Pay Attention to Small Details

Even when he was elected the president of a trade association, Kim made sure his staff were familiar with his working principles, and that they stuck to those principles. This is based on the fact that mistakes which would be forgivable on land can have fatal consequences at sea.

Take on New Challenges

Kim never stopped taking on new challenges, treating this as a part of his company's DNA. This was due to his philosophy that 'the essence of both life and business is change.' For Kim, change was a necessity rather than a choice.

You can only achieve results when you view the mountain from a strategic level, the forest from a tactical level and the trees from a practical level. The following is a summary of the 20 rules that Kim expects his staff to abide by.

1) Be well-acquainted with figures

Figures are the shortcut to understanding the current state of the business and what is happening in the field. They are the barometer through which interest is shown. Accordingly, Kim teaches people to "never compromise with numbers," because figures are the embodiment of truth, free from any emotion or falsehoods.

2) Be proficient in financial statements

Kim believes that nothing gives a more accurate picture of a company's current position than its financial statements.

3) Make regular checks

Kim believes that the success or failure of a business hinges on people, and that work should be "entrusted to people you can rely on." At the same time, he stresses the importance of having checks and balances. A system of checks and balances is not only for the company, but also for the sake of those who have been assigned work.

4) Be able to provide direction

It is a captain's job to catch fish. When a captain leads his crew to a location with fish, he must work harder and make more sacrifices than anyone else.

5) Do not flinch in the face of adversity

A great captain is able to perform well even in rough seas. Captains who have led only good ships do not know the true abilities or nature of their vessel, but captains who have worked on rickety old boats have the confidence to steer any ship.

Kim notes that while machines become worn out the more you use them, people become upgraded through experience. Ultimately, it is your thoughts and reactions that are the most important.

6) Opportunities always come after hardship

When times were tough, Kim told his staff to view the world in a positive light and be ready to grasp the opportunities that arrive after a tough ordeal.

7) The answer lies in the field

No matter the size of the problem, the answer can be found in the field. The reason Kim Jae-chul was able to survive while many other deep sea fishing companies experienced ups and downs was because of his wealth of hands-on experience.

8) Remember that things could collapse at any moment

Kim has never forgotten the fact that a business can come crashing down at any time, and he teaches his staff to remain equally vigilant through both his words and actions.

9) Keep a strict separation between public and private matters

This is a rule that Kim always followed. If an employee was unable to perform their function and generate value, they were removed from that position, even if that person was

Kim's own relative. Only those that proved their competence through results were able to keep their positions.

10) Conserve everything

The habit of thrift came naturally to Kim. "Scarcity builds character. Children should be taught at a young age to be careful with money. If a child learns to spend first, they will end in ruin," he stressed.

11) Ability is the key to survival

"Study hard!" Kim created a company culture of learning through attending lectures, reading and writing. Although he had a deep understanding of his trade, he never thought of himself as number one. Upgrading his knowledge and experience became part of his daily life.

12) Management hinges on your performance on stage and the ability of the actors

"Build a stage on which employees can get excited!" Kim compares a business to a stage, the members to theater actors, and the customers to an audience. This is his so-called 'stage theory of management.' This theory embodies the philosophy of putting on a positive performance for customers. Executives always remember the great example set by Kim Jae-chul.

13) Strive to become the best in your respective field

It is difficult to be good at everything, but you can become proficient in your field through selection and focus. In this respect, Kim's management philosophy is the 'mediocrity theory of management.' In order to reach a goal faster than a genius, you need mediocre people who are willing to work together and achieve synergy.

14) Leadership starts from self-regulation.

Those who are running behind the leader see only his actions, not his mouth. Leaders must be able to make sacrifices, devote themselves wholeheartedly, and have no weaknesses. Subordinates will only follow when you use your own abilities to achieve results.

15) Grab hold of opportunities when they appear

"Yesterday is yesterday, and today is today." Just because you caught a lot of fish today does not mean that tomorrow will be the same. Each occurrence is an independent event. Kim adopted a cautious approach to everything, but he would move like a bolt of lightning once he became certain of something. The seeds of a downfall begin to take root in the moment you lose your focus.

16) Be honest with yourself

Kim Jae-chul did not succeed because of his background. Instead, he succeeded through credit. This is why he told his employees "Never tell lies. Even if those above you are fooled, those below you know the truth."

17) Stand and face up to difficulties instead of avoiding them

"When you are confronted by a typhoon, trying to avoid the waves will only pull the boat into the eye of the storm." Even if it is tough, you must be willing to fight when you have to.

18) Make thorough preparations

Living at sea taught Kim the importance of making thorough preparations. People are prone to falling idle when left alone. The same holds true whether you are raising a child or motivating your subordinates.

19) You must have an upstanding set of values

Sharing your values with staff means teaching them why they are working and why they should strive to achieve excellence.

20) Reproach is a good medicine

As the Korean proverb says "Even a whale will dance when praised." It is true that praise and encouragement are an important part of leadership. However, Kim tends to use praise and encouragement in moderation. A leader must be willing to fiercely reprimand employees when necessary.

Kim Jae-chul's Lessons for CEOs

"A company grows in proportion to the CEO's competence." Kim believes that a company can succeed or fail depending on the competence and enthusiasm of its leaders.

The Seven Traits of a CEO

① A CEO must have an accurate understanding of the current state of the organization he is leading, and must focus on more than just the tangible. The essence of a company can only be found by observing that which is intangible.

② A CEO must be adept at management and mediation. Kim Jae-chul's Management

The areas to be managed can be defined as recruitment, distribution, education, evaluations, redeployment (rotation) and remuneration. A CEO is tasked with using finite resources to produce results. In particular, CEOs must be well-versed in the plan and know what is happening on the front lines.

③ An organization can only succeed when meritorious deeds are rewarded and no fault goes unpunished. Personal considerations should never play a role in personnel decisions. Training staff is another important mission for CEOs.

④ You must stand up to problems instead of avoiding them. As a manager, waves of problems will come to you in many forms. You must be able to enjoy the problem solving process and take responsibility for the outcomes.

⑤ A CEO must look to the future while making decisions in the present. If a CEO does not have a clear understanding of the company's goals and where it is headed, it will naturally lead to problems. This is why you must study.

⑥ Provide a stage on which staff can unleash their full potential. Staff performance depends on the actions of the CEO. It is true that a company can never become larger than the competence of its CEO permits.

⑦ A CEO must take responsibility for all outcomes.

Part V

Public Interest over Private Benefit

story 1

A Dream of Investing in Talent

"Investing in people, creating jobs and paying taxes. These are my three guiding principles in my life.

Although I had a number of bitter experiences while traveling overseas, it made me think that I could only exist, and the Korean people could only exist because of our country."

Kim's ideas on training staff were formed during his time as an officer-in-training, when he realized that he lacked the knowledge to carry even a 30-minute conversation with foreigners, and the culture shock he experienced in Paris and Rome while working for Korea Wonyang Fisheries. He recalls the feelings of lamentation and sadness as he thought

"What have we been doing in Korea while they left behind such great legacies?"

Investing in Staff

Training Programs in the Early Days

Kim began investing in people from his hometown in 1977, eight years after founding Dongwon. He set up the Gangjin Scholarship Association for the most underprivileged middle and high school students in Gangjin, which later developed into the Dongwon Educational Foundation that assisted college students around the country.

The Substantive Activities of Dongwon Educational Foundation

One of the notable features of the ads for recruiting scholarship students at Dongwon Educational Foundation is asking applicants to choose between two essay topics when writing their submission - 'my direction' and 'youth in modern times.' This embodies Kim's ideology of 'helping the nation stand tall by investing in people.' By 2014, the foundation had provided scholarships to 2,929 college students and 1,224 middle and high school students.

Reading and Writing Teaches People to Think

Kim firmly believes that "A path can be found through reading." Since 1989, the foundation has also hosted a writing contest. The first two iterations were called the 'Love for the Ocean Writing Contest,' with the following three based around the theme 'Love for the Earth,' and 'Love for My Family' for the remaining three contests.

Up until 2006, when this program came to an end, a total of 734,680 students had taken part across eight contests, with 5,924 receiving awards.

Dongwon Unveils the Bookworm Project

Based on the premise of encouraging people to pick up the habit of reading as children, the 'Dongwon Bookworm' project (Reading with Mom Campaign) was launched in 2007.

Every month, families with children aged 2-6 could apply to receive a free book, with a book distributed to 10,000 households each month for an annual total of 120,000. As of the end of 2014, one million books had been distributed through the program.

Kim plans to further expand this program, based on his belief that "You need to read in order to think, and you need to think in order to live a good life."

Youthful Experiences as a Lifelong Asset

Experiencing the World as Dongwon Global Explorers

Kim is currently experimenting with the 'Dongwon Global Explorers' program through the foundation. The term explorer refers to not only the outside world, but also exploring oneself.

This program, launched in 2012, encourages kids to "Turn the map upside down! Head out into the world!" This is a program that supports young people in following their dreams, providing opportunities to college students to expand their horizons and see more of the world. Students selected for the program are taken on a 14-day world tour across India, Indonesia, Tanzania, Argentina, Brazil, Kenya, the US and Europe, and write a report about the results of their projects.

Every year, hundreds of teams engage in fierce competition through preliminary contests and a final round to selected as one of the final 15. Reading the plans submitted by teams made up of 3-4 young people gives the impression that Korean youth have great potential after all.

Young people are encouraged to pursue four ideals.

① PASSION: Ignite a fire inside yourself.

② CHALLENGE: Take on something new.

③ CREATIVE: Think differently from the crowd.

④ GLOBAL: Embrace the world.

Just like Dongwon's corporate activities, the foundation's activities are made possible by Kim's continued interest in investing in people. Kim continues to achieve his childhood dreams by throwing seeds into the wilderness.

story 2

How to Invest in Staff

You must have a philosophy to follow in life.

"There are no large differences between people in terms of ability. The difference between winners and losers is mostly the amount of effort put in, and it doesn't seem that one's ancestry or educational background have a lot of influence. Those who are able to take action with their body and mind and work steadily towards a goal will ultimately be victorious." This is a quote from Kim Jae-chul.

The Importance of Having a Philosophy

Hard work is of no use unless one makes their own

decisions. Kim always stresses the importance of philosophy to his staff, with the goal of developing a healthy attitude towards life and work.

Dongwon's Philosophy and Guidelines for Action

① Passionate action: Act with passion and enthusiasm

② Clear purpose: Actively take on challenges and have a clear goal

③ Communication: Communicate and cooperate with one another

④ Quantification: Make results quantifiable and check the gains or losses yourself

⑤ Taking action: Take pleasure in performing your work

⑥ A socially necessary enterprise: Serve as a pillar of your country and society

Kim says that he cannot repeat the mantra "Do it thoroughly. Do it with conviction. Do it until completion" often enough.

Listening, Reading and Writing - The Foundation of Investing in Staff

Forty Years of the Thursday Seminar

Dongwon Group's 'Thursday Seminar' tradition has been ongoing for 40 years and is currently heading towards its 2,000th lecture. Even now, over every four week period the company holds one guest lecture with an invited speaker, one research topic presentation by executives and staff and two team-based seminars on current issues.

Reading Helps to Grasp Business Opportunities and Boost Creativity

Kim holds a firm belief that developing the capabilities of executives and staff is both crucial to corporate success and the core of individual success. 'Reading management,' which was first introduced in 2002, encourages employees to write down the things they read until they are able to turn it into their own. Writing promotes organized thinking and the ability to apply what one has learned.

story 3

The Path to Industry Development

The Launch of the Ministry of Maritime Affairs and Fisheries

Among Kim's numerous contributions to the development of the maritime industry, his greatest feat was playing a pivotal role in the launch of the Ministry of Maritime Affairs and Fisheries, a long-cherished wish of industry members.

The Enactment of the Framework Act on Marine Development and the Formation of the Ocean Development Research Society

When the 'Committee for the Promotion of the Framework Act on Marine Development' was launched as a research body, Kim Jae-chul was inducted as the committee chair in the first meeting. The committee's efforts culminated in the enactment of the Framework Act on Marine Development in 1987.

The Ocean Development Research Society was also founded to handle maritime affairs, which were dispersed across numerous government departments, and provide a more systematic approach. Kim not only financial support to the society, but also played a leading role in academic research.

During the process of launching the Ministry of Maritime Affairs and Fisheries under the Kim Young-sam administration, National Assembly member Park Gwan-yong (Chief Presidential Secretary and Speaker of the National Assembly) played an important role. When Park was serving on the National Assembly's Educational Affairs and Communication Committee as an administrator for the opposition party, Kim Jae-chul, who was the head of the alumni association at Busan National Maritime University at the time, gave him a logical explanation as to why his alma mater should be turned into a general university.

When Park heard what Kim had to say, he couldn't help but

think "This man is very different from other businessmen." When Kim was certain he was fighting for a justified cause, he threw his entire weight behind persuading people, and did not easily take no for an answer. Just like that, Busan National Maritime University was promoted to regular university status.

Earning a Reputation on Merit

In 1993, the Kim Young-sam administration set up a committee for administrative reform. Park Gwan-yong, who was Chief Presidential Secretary at the time, believed that the committee should not revolve about public officials with regulatory authority, and ensured that three civilians were added to the committee. One of them was Kim Jae-chul.

From that point on, Park said that whenever he wanted to get an accurate picture of what was going on in the world, all he had to do was sit down with Kim Jae-chul. In this sense, Kim was highly revered in officialdom, which is believed to have been behind his appointment as chairman of the Korea International Trade Association when the Kim Dae-jung government came to power.

story 4

The Path towards the Nation and Public Benefit

Revolutionizing the Trade Association

Whenever Kim was delegated a new task, his first question would be "What are my duties?" After gathering his thoughts, he would carry out the task in line with his personal philosophy and methodology.

However, this came at a cost when performing public service. His external commitments caused him to neglect his own business because they divided his time, attention and energy. However, Kim remained enthusiastically involved in a number of other projects including serving as the Chairman of the Korea International Trade Association, setting up the Jang Bogo Memorial Project Enterprise and bidding for the Yeosu World Expo.

In 1999, the Korea International Trade Association was swept up by a mountainous wave while Kim was at the helm. The sudden change in the trade environment brought about by the World Trade Organization (WTO) system led to amendments to the Foreign Trade Act that abolished the approval system for exports and imports and did away with funds. This led to a financial crisis for the association.

Kim knew what the association had to do in order to achieve fiscal independence. The 'Management Innovation Report Using the Trade Association as a Case Study' written by Gu Bon-hyeong contains a vivid description of Kim's reforms.

The Principles of Reform

Kim Jae-chul put forward five principles under the banner of organizational reform.

① We must become an organization that could accurately assess customer needs.

② We must broaden our income streams and reduce

unnecessary costs.

③ We must manage the association in accordance with corporate management principles.

④ We must work hard to boost per capita productivity.

⑤ All accounting must be transparent.

Alongside these revolutionary changes to the trade association, Kim conducted major surgery on the organization's hardware and software.

① Seek to change the attitude and work methods of executives and staff by introducing the concept of cost of production.

② Make quantitative assessments of cost savings and customer satisfaction by training executives and staff to be more proficient in finance and accounting, which are basic business concepts, and instilling a business mindset.

③ Introduce the 'Tuesday Forum' to help drive personal development on an individual level, and make this part of the trade association's culture by making sure that the Chairman attends every session for four years.

As a result of these changes, the association reduced its number of staff by 32.2%, the highest figure amongst all economic organizations. Thanks to these efforts, the association became more financially secure, cut staff numbers from 504 to 239, and raised the proportion of staff with a Master's degree or higher to 43.5% by hiring more young people. In an interview at the end of his tenure as chairman, Kim Jae-chul said the following.

"The staff at the association no longer work for the sake of working. They are now focused on getting results. Although I feel sad to have let so many people go as part of this process, I prefer to use the term 'metabolism' instead of restructuring. Innovation is impossible without a sense of duty."

After helping the association achieve harmonious development, and elevate its role and standing, Kim stepped down as chairman after seven years in 2006.

Spreading the Word About Jang Bogo, the King of the Seas

Jang Bogo, an Entrepreneur Who Was Ahead of His Time

The project to shed new light on the life of Jang Bogo began in 1999 when the Ministry of Maritime Affairs and Fisheries formed the 'Committee for the Promotion of the Jang Bogo Re-exploration Project,' which consisted of representatives from academia and related industries. On this occasion, Kim Jae-chul was once again selected to chair the committee. The Jang Bogo Memorial Project Enterprise was later formed, with Kim serving as the chairman of the board for 11 years.

In his time, Jang Bogo was a master of international trade, successfully connecting the Southeast Asian and Indian sea routes to create a trade network between the East and West. During this period, he also helped to create greater added value for Korean trade by exporting Goryeo celadon to Japan and Islamic countries. Kim Jae-chul believed that Korea should use Jang Bogo's spirit as a benchmark by learning from his achievements. He launched the 'Jang Bogo Research Society' to conduct more systematic research, and published 63 books of 42 types over a ten year period, as well as 25 books of 17 different types for sale.

On one occasion, President Kim Dae-jung approached Kim with a proposal. "The drama 'Taejo Wang Geon' seems very popular these days, so how about producing a drama themed around Jang Bogo?"

Kim replied "I think it would be difficult to produce such a drama right now. If we try to make it popular, it could undermine historical accuracy. How about filming a drama when we are better prepared?"

The president told him to do just that.

Once the meeting had finished, one minister was shocked by what he had seen. "Mr. Kim, how could you turn down a request from the president?" he asked. But irrespective of who he was speaking to, the habit of carefully considering a proposal and then coming to a rational conclusion was deeply ingrained in the mind of Kim Jae-chul. At the time, Kim remembered a drama based on Heo Jun (a famous Korean doctor) written by author Choi In-ho. After thorough research, Choi was tasked with writing the novel, and a series of short stories titled 'God of the Sea' that depicted the life of Jang Bogo was published in the JoongAng Ilbo over a two year period from July 2000.

In January 2003, KBS screened a special edition 51-episode drama series with the same title. Even today, the sets for Cheonghaejin (an old Korean military headquarters) and Sillabang are still around in Wando-gun, and the sites were recently used for the filming of the movie 'The Admiral: Roaring Currents.'

In an era marked by a new maritime order in the 21st century, the Jang Bogo Memorial Project Enterprise has helped to pass down Korea's sea culture through generations as an important part of the nation's psyche by raising awareness about the importance of the sea and shedding new light on Jang Bogo's experiences at sea from a modern perspective.

Lending Weight to Yeosu's World Expo Bid

Although President Roh Moo-hyun played an active part in bringing the expo to Korea, the bid was ultimately won by Shanghai in the World Expo's General Assembly in Monaco in 2002. Korea once again made a bid in 2006, but it was a tough nut to crack.

With His Knowledge of the Seas, Kim Jae-chul is the Right Man for the Job

At the time Kim was appointed as the chair of the Bidding Committee, he had already finished working at KITA. Although he had been asked several times, on each occasion he turned down the request. The President invited Kim to the Blue House,

But he arrived late because traffic congestion was particularly bad that day. However, Kim was surprised to see that the President and his aides were all waiting outside to greet him. In the face of such a great demonstration of respect, Kim had no choice but to leave the decision to the President and accept the position as leader of the Bidding Committee.

Reforming the Bidding Committee

In the beginning, the Bidding Committee was a disorderly group. Kim began by implementing stronger discipline and injecting greater enthusiasm into the organization. He attended every meeting in person and the committee began to take shape. Beginning with a personal donation of two billion KRW from the chairman, the committee was able to raise ten billion KRW in funds.

Although Kim had turned down the position several times, he eventually chose to accept based on his lifelong belief that "Raising public awareness about the importance of the sea will be good for the Korean people."

Claiming Victory in the Bidding War

"Once you join the race, you have to win." Before the General Assembly was held, Kim recruited the leaders of Samsung, LG SK, Hanjin and other conglomerates, including Hyundai Motors CEO Chung Mong-koo, to visit member countries alongside the committee. They demonstrated great enthusiasm, circling the globe 42 times in total. As a result of these efforts, Yeosu was chosen to host the 2012 World Expo. Kim had a solid grasp of what it took to win.

His secret to success was mobilizing Korea's embassies and diplomatic offices abroad to join the effort, and placing competent leaders in charge of the supporting committees behind the scenes. As a result of his achievements, Kim was awarded the Order of Civil Merit, Peony Medal, the highest honor that can be bestowed on a civilian.

The Korean Peninsula Looks Different if You Turn the Map Upside Down

In his 2000 book 'If You Turn the Map Upside Down, You See the Future of Korea,' Kim Jae-chul wrote the following.

"I recommend turning the map upside down to look at the world. The earth is round. There is actually no such thing as the top or bottom, but we tend to think this way when we look at a map of the world. My suggestion to look at the world upside down means changing the way we think.

For a long time, we have been obsessed with the idea that the Eurasian continent lives to the north of the Korean Peninsula, but it's a different story if we turn the map upside down.

Instead of being a peninsula at the far east side of the Eurasian continent, the Korean Peninsula becomes a land of great prosperity that links Eurasia to the vast Pacific Ocean. In other words, the Korean Peninsula is a key strategic location that serves as the gateway to Northeast Asia."

Part VI

The Significance of Kim Jae-chul in Economic and Business History

story 1

Economic Significance

Let's take a look at the specific ways in which Kim Jae-chul's actions contributed to Korea's economy, and the significance of those actions.

1) A leading role in building the nation through exports

In the 1970s, Kim was a key figure in helping Korea develop through exports.

2) A shining example of the entrepreneurial spirit

Kim read the trends of the times and served as the cornerstone for the development of the deep sea fishing industry.

3) Established the idea that companies should not make a loss

As a businessman, Kim never placed a burden on the state.

4) The driving force behind the launch of the Ministry of Maritime Affairs and Fisheries

Kim made an active contribution to the establishment of the new ministry.

5) A leader of the first generation of venture entrepreneurs

In a broad sense, he represented the first generation of venture companies.

6) An embodiment of the pioneering spirit

Kim always took the lead in seeking out new fishing grounds, new fishing techniques and new technologies.

7) The provider of a new source of protein

Marine products served as a new source of protein for the Korean people.

8) A great illuminator who taught the importance of harnessing the oceans

Kim reminds us of the sea's importance.

9) Establishing a new image of a model taxpayer

Kim served as a role model for society by faithfully paying his gift tax.

10) An exemplary case study in reforming public entities

Kim demonstrated how to achieve innovation in non-profit organizations.

story 2

Business Significance

1) Dongwon Industries is the only deep sea fishing company founded in the 1960s that still exists today.

2) Kim developed from a leader in the deep sea fishing industry to a leader in the general foods sector.

3) Kim built on the foundation he had established in the deep sea fishing business to find a new avenue of growth in the financial sector.

4) Kim created a new future for the deep sea fishing industry by pioneering tuna purse seining.

5) Kim is an exemplary case of ethical corporate governance and righteous management through the introduction of a holding company structure.

6) Kim successfully entered the global market by acquiring StarKist.

7) As a former ship captain, Kim successfully built a large corporation.

8) Kim contributed to development in the fishing industry through his pioneering spirit.

9) Kim is a fighter who emerged victorious even in the worst of circumstances.

10) Kim put forward a model for investing in staff.

11) Kim sets a good example through his commitment to righteous management

Epilogue

Life is about Finding a Way to Win Even When Times are Tough

Kim Jae-chul's life can be described as 'a life well-lived' or 'a moving story with a lot of lessons.' What is the significance of being born into an era of hardship? One cannot speak about Kim's life without bringing up responsibility.

I have often wondered "Why do we have so few records to show for the things we do?" In particular, those in the business world should take the time to organize their memoirs, for both their own sake and future generations.

I was tasked with writing this book because I too believed in this need. I hope that this book will serve not only as a record of Kim Jae-chul's life and business, but also as a reminder to future generations of how previous generations built the Korea of today.

Finally, I hope that the stories contained in this book will provide wisdom and serve as a lesson for people living in the current era. The burdens of life may be heavy, but we cannot put them down.

In fact, as the burden becomes heavier, we must resolve with all our heart to strive for excellence. While Kim Jae-chul began his life with empty hands, I believe the most important part of his journey is not what he achieved, but the the process through which he reached those achievements.

Writing this book was an enjoyable journey. It was an opportunity to learn something very valuable as a humble human being.

Gong Byung-ho (Author)

THROUGH THE WAVES:

Life and Business Stories of
Captain Kim Jae-chul